"THE SPIRIT OF THE LORD IS MOVING IN THESE DAYS"

So proclaimed Smith Wigglesworth more than 40 years ago. Here, in this inspiring book, are some of the words he spoke as he led untold thousands to Christ, all over the world.

His fervent and unyielding belief gave his message a meaning and power that few men of God have ever achieved. The words of this simple and ever-joyous man are fresh and vital today—and so will be . . . for all time, for all men.

EVER INCREASING FAITH

Smith Wigglesworth

Revised Edition

GOSPEL PUBLISHING HOUSE • Springfield, Missouri

02–0494

Ever Increasing Faith Copyright Page

© 1924 by Smith Wigglesworth
Revised Edition © 1971 by Gospel Publishing House, Springfield,
Missouri 65802-1894. All rights reserved.

TWENTY-FIFTH PRINTING, 1992

ISBN: 0-88243-494-2

Printed in the United States of America

Foreword

Smith Wigglesworth, the twentieth century "Apostle of Faith," was a legend in his time. It could be said of him, as of those in the Early Church, God bore witness of his ministry "with signs and wonders, and with divers miracles, and gifts of the Holy Ghost, according to His will."

Here was an uneducated plumber of Bradford, England—a highly unlikely candidate for a worldwide ministry—but God took him and used him in a very unique manner.

Wigglesworth was born in 1859, in a humble shack in Menston, Yorkshire, England. At eight years of age he was converted in a Wesleyan Methodist meeting which he attended with his devout grandmother. He in turn was instrumental in his own mother's conversion. When he was 13, his parents moved to Bradford, and then three years later he began working with the Salvation Army. Even as a teen-ager Wigglesworth was zealous to see others won to the Lord. When he was twenty, Wigglesworth moved to Liverpool where he ministered to scores of poor children in dock sheds. Hundreds of them were saved. Later, he returned to Bradford where he opened his own plumbing business. A short time after he returned to Bradford he married Polly Featherstone, who was a great soul winner herself. In the early years of their marriage it was Mrs. Wigglesworth who was the preacher and Smith the personal worker at the little mission they operated in Bradford.

In 1907, when he was 48, Wigglesworth's life pattern was dramatically changed. From a relatively small, part-time ministry in Bradford, God thrust him out to a world-wide evangelistic ministry. As he told it many times later, the remarkable change came when he received the baptism in the Holy Spirit. From that day to the end of his life, Smith Wigglesworth was a spiritual dynamo. Calls for his ministry—untrained though he was—came from all over the world. Through his mass meetings he led literally thousands to Christ; many were introduced to the Pentecostal experience; his faith-inspiring messages brought healing to untold numbers. He was untiring in his efforts to minister—often preaching three times a day and witnessing wherever he had opportunity.

Ever Increasing Faith is a collection of eighteen messages Wigglesworth preached in different parts of the world. He had no plans to write them for publication, but they were taken down in shorthand and later published. The book was first published in 1924 and has since been through many reprintings and has been translated into many languages.

Smith Wigglesworth went to be with the Lord in his 87th year. His critics are gone and forgotten, but the simple, uneducated plumber from Bradford continues to bring sinners to Christ and inspire faith for healing through these messages.

With the passing of time certain phrases fall into disuse. For the sake of clarity the publisher has issued this revised edition. The message of Smith Wigglesworth remains unchanged—only certain expressions throughout the text that would possibly be misunderstood have been revised.

WAYNE E. WARNER, EDITOR

Contents

1

Have Faith in God

"For verily I say unto you, That whosoever shall say unto this mountain, Be thou removed, and be thou cast into the sea; and shall not doubt in his heart, but shall believe that those things which he saith shall come to pass; he shall have whatsoever he saith. Therefore I say unto you, What things soever ye desire when ye pray, believe that ye receive them, and ye shall have them" (Mark 11:23, 24).

These are days when we need to have our faith strengthened, when we need to know God. God has designed that the just shall live by faith. Any man can be changed by faith, no matter how he may be fettered. I know that God's word is sufficient. One word from Him can change a nation. His word is from everlasting to everlasting. Is is through the entrance of this everlasting Word, this incorruptible seed, that we are born again and come into this wonderful salvation. Man cannot live by bread alone, but must live by every word that proceedeth out of the mouth of God. This is the food of faith. "Faith cometh by hearing, and hearing by the Word of God."

Everywhere men are trying to discredit the Bible and take from it all the miraculous. One preacher says, "Well, you know, Jesus arranged beforehand to have that colt tied where it was, and for the men to say just what they did." I tell you God can arrange everything without going near. He can plan for you,

9

and when He plans for you, all is peace. All things are possible if you will believe.

Another preacher said, "It was an easy thing for Jesus to feed the people with five loaves. The loaves were so big in those days that it was a simple matter to cut them into a thousand pieces each." But He forgot that one little boy brought those five loaves all the way in his lunch basket. There is nothing impossible with God. All the impossibility is with us when we measure God by the limitations of our unbelief.

We have a wonderful God, a God whose ways are past finding out and whose grace and power are limitless. I was in Belfast one day and saw one of the brethren of the assembly. He said to me, "Wigglesworth, I am troubled. I have had a good deal of sorrow during the past five months. I had a woman in my assembly who could always pray the blessing of heaven down on our meetings. She is an old woman, but her presence is always an inspiration. But five months ago she fell and broke her thigh. The doctors put her into a plaster cast, and after five months they broke the cast. But the bones were not properly set, and so she fell and broke the thigh again."

He took me to her house, and there was a woman lying in a bed on the right hand side of the room. I said to her, "Well, what about it now?" She said, "They have sent me home incurable. The doctors say that I am so old that my bones won't knit. There is no nutriment in my bones and they could never do anything for me, and they say I shall have to lie in bed for the rest of my life." I said to her, "Can you believe God?" She replied, "Yes, ever since I heard that you had come to Belfast my faith has been quickened. If you will pray, I will believe. I know there is no power on earth that can make the bones of my thigh knit, but I know there is nothing impossible with God." I said, "Do you believe He will meet you now?" She answered, "I do."

It is grand to see people believe God. God knew all about this leg and that it was broken in two places. I said to the woman, "When I pray, something will happen." Her husband was sitting there; he had been in his chair for four years and could not walk a step. He called out, "I don't believe. I won't believe. You will never get me to believe." I said, "All right," and laid my hands on his wife in the name of the Lord Jesus. The moment hands were laid upon her the power of God went right through her and she cried out, "I'm healed." I said, "I'm not going to assist you to rise. God will do it all." She rose and walked up and down the room, praising God.

The old man was amazed at what had happened to his wife, and he cried out, "Make me walk, make me walk." I said to him, "You old sinner, repent." He cried out, "Lord, You know I never meant what I said. You know I believe." I don't think he meant what he said; anyhow the Lord was full of compassion. If He marked our sins, where would any of us be? If we will meet the conditions, God will always meet us. If we believe, all things are possible. I laid my hands on him and the power went right through the old man's body; and those legs, for the first time in four years, received power to carry his body, and he walked up and down and in and out. He said, "O what great things God has done for us tonight!"

"What things soever ye desire, when ye pray, believe that ye receive them, and ye shall have them." Desire toward God, and you will have desires from God; and He will meet you on the line of those desires when you reach out in simple faith.

A man came to me in one of my meetings who had seen other people healed and wanted to be healed, too. He explained that his arm had been fixed in a certain position for many years and he could not move it. "Got any faith?" I asked. He said he had a lot of faith. After prayer he was able to swing his arm round and round. But he was not satisfied and complained, "I feel a little bit of trouble just there," pointing to a certain place. "Do you know what is the trouble with you?" He answered, "No." I said, "Imperfect faith." *"What things soever ye desire, when ye pray, believe that ye receive them, and ye shall have them."*

Did you believe before you were saved? So many people would be saved, but they want to feel saved first. There was never a man who felt saved before he believed. God's plan is always this: If you will believe, you shall see the glory of God. I believe God wants to bring us all to a definite place of unswerving faith and confidence in Himself.

Jesus here uses the figure of a mountain. Why does He say a mountain? Because if faith can remove a mountain, it can remove anything. The plan of God is so marvelous that if you will only believe, all things are possible.

There is one special phrase to which I want to call your attention, "And shall not doubt in his heart." The heart is the mainspring. See that young man and young woman. They have fallen in love at first sight. In a short while there is a deep affection and a strong heart love, the one toward the other. What is a heart of love? A heart of faith. Faith and love are kin. In the measure that that young man and that young woman love one another they are true. One may go to the North and the other to the South, but because of their love they will be true to each other.

It is the same when there is a deep love in the heart toward the Lord Jesus Christ. In this new life into which God has brought us, Paul tells us that we have become dead to the law by the body of Christ, that we should be *married to another*, even to Him who is raised from the dead. God brings us into a place of perfect love and perfect faith. A man who is born of God is brought into an inward affection, a loyalty to the Lord Jesus that shrinks from anything impure. You see the purity of a man and woman when there is a deep natural affection between them; they disdain the very thought of either of them being untrue. I say that in the measure that a man has faith in Jesus, he is pure. He that believes that Jesus is the Christ overcomes the world. It is a faith that works by love.

Just as we have heart fellowship with our Lord, our faith cannot be daunted. We cannot doubt in our hearts. There comes, as we go on with God, a wonderful association, an impartation of His very life and nature within. As we read His Word and believe the promises that He has so graciously given to us, we are made partakers of His very essence and life. The Lord is made to us a Bridegroom, and we are His bride. His words to us are spirit and life, transforming us and changing us, expelling that which is natural and bringing in that which is divine.

It is impossible to comprehend the love of God as we think on natural lines. We must have the revelation from the Spirit of God. God giveth liberally. He that asketh, receiveth. God is willing to bestow on us all things that pertain to life and godliness. Oh, it was the love of God that brought Jesus. And it is this same love that helps you and me to believe. In every weakness God will be your strength. You who need His touch, remember that He loves you. Look, wretched, helpless, sick one, away to the God of all grace whose very essence is love, who delights to give liberally all the inheritance of life and strength and power that you are in need of.

In Switzerland the Lord was graciously working and healing many of the people. I was staying with Brother Reuss of Goldiwil and two policemen were sent to arrest me. The charge was that I was healing the people without a license. Mr. Reuss said to them, "I am sorry that he is not here just now. He is holding a meeting about two miles away, but before you arrest him let me show you something."

Brother Reuss took the two policemen down to one of the lower parts of that district to a house with which they were familiar, for they had often gone to that place to arrest a certain woman who was repeatedly put in prison because she was often engaged in drunken brawls. Brother Reuss took them to this woman and said, "This is one of the many cases of blessing that have come through the ministry of the man you have come to arrest. This woman came to our meeting in a drunken condition Her body was broken, for she was ruptured in two places. While she was drunk, the evangelist laid his hands on her and asked God to heal her and deliver her." The policemen had a warrant for my arrest, but they said with disgust, "Let the doctors do this kind of thing." They turned and went away and that was the last we heard of them.

We have a Jesus that heals the brokenhearted, who lets the captives go free, who saves the very worst. Dare you, *dare you* spurn this glorious Gospel of God for spirit, soul and body? Dare you spurn this grace? I realize that this full gospel has in great measure been hid, this Gospel that brings liberty, this Gospel that brings souls out of bondage, this Gospel that brings perfect health to the body, this Gospel of entire salvation. Listen again to this word of Him who left the glory to bring us this great salvation, "Verily I say unto you, That whosoever shall say unto this mountain, Be thou removed, . . . he shall have whatsoever he saith." *Whatsoever!*

I realize that God can never bless us on the lines of being hardhearted, critical, or unforgiving. This will hinder faith quicker than anything. I remember being at a meeting where there were some people tarrying for the Baptism, seeking for cleansing—for the moment a person is cleansed the Spirit will fall. There was one man with eyes red from weeping bitterly. He said to me, "I shall have to leave. It is no good my staying without I change things. I have written a letter to my brother-in-law and filled it with hard words, and this thing must first be straightened out." He went home and told his wife, "I'm going to write a letter to your brother and ask him to forgive me for writing to him the way I did." "You fool!" she said. "Never mind," he replied, "this is between God and me, and it has got to be cleared away." He wrote the letter and came again, and immediately God filled him with the Spirit.

I believe there are a great many people who would be healed, but they are harboring things in their hearts that are as a blight. Let these things go. Forgive and the Lord will forgive you. There are many good people, people that mean well, but they have no power to do anything for God. There is just some little thing that came in their hearts years ago, and their faith has been paralyzed since. Bring everything to the light. God will sweep it all away if you will let Him. Let the precious blood of Christ cleanse from all sin. If you will but believe, God will meet you and bring into your lives the sunshine of His love.

HEALINGS IN NEW ZEALAND

We have received a few testimonies of those healed in the meeting conducted by Brother Smith Wigglesworth at Wellington, New Zealand. Mrs. E. Curtis of Christchurch, New Zealand, was suffering with septic poisoning. She had become only a skeleton and the doctors could do nothing for her. She had agonizing pains all day and all night. She was healed immediately when prayer was made for her. She states that for the past sixteen years she has been a martyr to pain but is now wonderfully well. Another testified to healing deafness, goiter, adenoids and bad eyesight. Another testified to healing of double curvature of the spine from infancy, hip disease, weak heart, leg lengthened three inches, which grew normal like the other leg. It was also three inches less in circumference. She wore a large boot but now walks on even feet, the large boot having been discarded. Another was healed from goiter.—*The Pentecostal Evangel.*

2

Deliverance to the Captives

Scripture Reading, Luke 4:1-20.

Our precious Lord Jesus has everything for everybody. Forgiveness of sin, healing of diseases, and the fullness of the Spirit all come from one source—from the Lord Jesus Christ. Hear Him who is the same yesterday, today, and forever as He announces the purpose for which He came: "The Spirit of the Lord is upon me, because he hath anointed me to preach the gospel to the poor; he hath sent me to heal the broken-hearted, to preach deliverance to the captives, and recovering of sight to the blind, to set at liberty them that are bruised, to preach the acceptable year of the Lord."

Jesus was baptized by John in the Jordan, and the Holy Spirit descended in a bodily shape like a dove upon Him. Being full of the Holy Ghost, He was led by the Spirit into the wilderness, there to come off more than conqueror over the arch enemy. Then He returned in the power of the Spirit to Galilee and preached in the synagogues, and at last He came to His old home town—Nazareth, where He announced His mission in the words I have quoted above. For a brief while He ministered on the earth, and then gave His life a ransom for all. But God raised Him from the dead. And before He returned to heaven He told His disciples that they too should receive the power of the Holy Spirit. Thus, through them, His gracious ministry would continue. This power of the Holy Spirit was not only for a few apostles, but even for them that are afar off, even as many as our God should call (Acts 2:39), even for us in this twentieth century. Some ask, "But was not this power just for the privileged few in the first century?" No. Read the Master's great commission as recorded by Mark, and you will see it is for *them that believe.*

After I received the Baptism of the Holy Spirit (and I know that I received, for the Lord gave me the Spirit in just the same way as He gave Him to the disciples at Jerusalem), I sought the mind of the Lord as to why I was baptized. One day I came home from work and went into the house and my wife asked me, "Which way did you come in?" I told her I came in the back door. She said, "There is a woman upstairs who has brought an old man of eighty to be prayed for. He is raving up there and a great crowd is outside the front door, ringing the doorbell and wanting to know what is going on in the house." The Lord quietly whispered, "This is what I baptized you for."

I carefully opened the door of the room where the man was, desiring to be obedient to what my Lord would say to me. The man was crying and shouting in distress, "I am lost! I am lost! I have committed the unpardonable sin. I am lost! I am lost!" My wife said, "Dad, what shall we do?" The Spirit of the Lord moved me to cry out, "Come out, thou lying spirit." In a moment the evil spirit went, and the man was free. Deliverance to the captives! And the Lord said to me, "This is what I baptized you for."

There is a place where God, through the power of the Holy Spirit, reigns supreme in our lives. The Spirit reveals, unfolds, takes of the things of Christ and shows them to us, and prepares us to be more than a match for Satanic forces.

When Nicodemus came to Jesus he said, "We know that thou art a teacher come from God: for no man can do these miracles that thou doest, except God be with him." Jesus said to him, "Verily, verily I say unto thee, Except a man be born again, he cannot see the kingdom of God." Nicodemus was impressed by the miracles wrought; and Jesus pointed out the necessity of a miracle being wrought with every man who would see the Kingdom. When a man is born of God, is brought from darkness to light, a mighty miracle is wrought. Jesus saw every touch by God as a miracle, and so we may expect to see miracles wrought today. It is wonderful to have the Spirit of the Lord upon us. I would rather have the Spirit of God on me for five minutes than to receive a million dollars.

Do you see how Jesus mastered the devil in the wilderness? Jesus knew He was the Son of God and Satan came along with an "if." How many times has Satan come to you this way? He says, "After all, you may be deceived. You know you really are not a child of God." If the devil says you are not saved, it is a pretty sure sign that you are. When he tells you that you are not healed, it may be taken as good evidence that the Lord has sent His word and healed you. The devil knows that if he can capture your thought life, he has won a mighty victory over you. His great business is injecting thoughts, but if you are pure and holy you will instantly shrink from them. God wants us to let the mind that was in Christ Jesus, that pure, holy, humble mind of Christ, be in us.

I come across people everywhere I go who are held bound by deceptive conditions, and these conditions have come about simply because they have allowed the devil to make their minds the place of his stronghold. How are we to guard against this? The Lord has provided us with weapons that are mighty through God to the pulling down of these strongholds of the enemy, and by means of which every thought shall be brought into captivity to the obedience of Christ. The blood of Jesus Christ and His mighty name are an antidote to all the subtle seeds of unbelief that Satan would sow in your minds.

In the first chapter of Acts we see that Jesus gave commandment to the disciples that they should wait for the promise of the Father, and He told them that not many days later they would be baptized with the Holy Spirit. Luke tells us that he had written his former treatise concerning all that Jesus began both to do and teach. The ministry of Christ did not end at the cross, but the Acts and the Epistles give us accounts of what He continued to do and teach through those whom He indwelt. And our blessed Lord Jesus is still alive and continues His ministry through those who are filled with His Spirit. He is still healing the brokenhearted and delivering the captives through those on whom He places His Spirit.

I was traveling one day on a railway train in Sweden. At one station there boarded the train an elderly woman with her daughter. The woman's expression was so troubled that I asked about her. I heard that she was going to the hospital to have her leg taken off. She began to weep as she told that the doctors had said there was no hope for her unless her leg was amputated. She was seventy years old. I said to my interpreter, "Tell her that Jesus can heal her." The instant this was said to her, it was as though a veil was taken off her face; it became so light. We stopped at another station and the car filled up with people. There was a rush of men to board the train and the devil said, "You're done." But I knew I had the best proposition, for hard things are always opportunities to get to the Lord *more glory* when He manifests His power. Every trial is a blessing. There have been times when I have been pressed through circumstances and it seemed as if a dozen railroad engines were going over me, but I have found that the hardest things are just lifting places into the grace of God. We have such a lovely Jesus. He always proves Himself to be such a mighty Deliverer. He never fails to plan the best things for us.

The train began moving and I crouched down, and in the name of Jesus commanded the disease to leave. The old lady cried, "I'm healed. I know I'm healed." She stamped her leg and said, "I'm going to prove it." So when we stopped at another station she marched up and down and shouted, "I'm not going to the hospital." Once again our wonderful Jesus had proven Himself a Healer of the brokenhearted, a Deliverer of one that was bound.

At one time I was so bound that no human power could help me. My wife thought I would die. There was no help. At that time I had just had a faint glimpse of Jesus as the Healer. For six months I had been suffering from appendicitis, occasionally getting temporary relief. I went to the mission of which I was pastor, but I was brought to the floor in awful agony, and they brought me home to my bed. All night I was praying, pleading for deliverance, but none came. My wife was sure it was my home call and sent for a physician. He said that there was no possible chance for me—my body was too weak. Having had the appendicitis for six months, my whole system was drained, and because of that, he thought that it was too late for an operation. He left my wife in a state of broken-heartedness.

After he left, there came to our door a young man and an elderly woman. I knew that she was a woman of real prayer. They came upstairs to my room. This young man jumped on the bed and commanded the evil spirit to come out of me. He shouted, "Come out, you devil; I command you to come out in the name of Jesus!" There was no chance for an argument, or for me to tell him that I would never believe that there was a devil inside of me. The thing had to go in the name of Jesus, and it went, and I was instantly healed.

I arose and dressed and went downstairs. I was still in the plumbing business, and I asked my wife, "Is there any work in? I am all right now, and I am going to work." I found there was a certain job to be done and I picked up my tools and went off to do it. Just after I left, the doctor came in, put his plug hat down in the hall, and walked up to the bedroom. But the invalid was not there. "Where is Mr. Wigglesworth?" he asked. "Oh, doctor, he's gone out to work." said my wife. "You'll never see him alive again," said the doctor; "they'll bring him back a corpse."

Well, I'm the corpse.

Since that time, in many parts of the world, the Lord has given me the privilege of praying for people with appendicitis; and I have seen a great many people up and dressed within a quarter of an hour from the time I prayed for them. We have a living Christ who is willing to meet people on every line.

A number of years ago I met Brother D. W. Kerr and he gave me a letter of introduction to a brother in Zion City named Cook. I took his letter to Brother Cook, and he said, "God has sent you here." He gave

me the addresses of six people and asked me to go
and pray for them and meet him again at noon. When
I returned he told me about a young man who was to
be married the following Monday. His sweetheart was
in Zion City dying of appendicitis. I went to the
house and found that the physician had just been
there and had given her no hope. The mother was
nearly distracted and was pulling her hair and saying,
"Is there no deliverance!" I said to her, "Woman, believe God and your daughter will be healed and be
up and dressed in fifteen minutes." But the mother
went on screaming.

They took me into the bedroom, and I prayed for
the girl and commanded the evil spirit to depart in
the name of Jesus. She cried, "I am healed." I said to
her, "Do you want me to believe that you are healed?
If you are healed, get up." She said, "I'll get up." In
less than ten minutes the doctor came in. He wanted
to know what had happened. She said, "A man came
in and prayed for me, and I'm healed." The doctor
pressed his finger right in the place that had been so
sore, and the girl neither moaned nor cried. He said,
"This is God." It made no difference whether he ac-
knowledged it or not, I knew that God had worked.
Our God is real in saving and healing power today.
Our Jesus is just the same, yesterday, and today, and
forever. He saves and heals today just as of old, and
He wants to be your Saviour and your Healer.

Oh, if you would only believe God! What would
happen? The greatest things. Some have never tasted
the grace of God, have never had the peace of God.
Unbelief robs them of these blessings. It is possible to
hear and yet not conceive the truth. It is possible to
read the Word and not share in the life it brings. It is
necessary for us to have the Holy Spirit to unfold the

Word and bring to us the life that is Christ. We can never fully understand the wonders of this redemption until we are full of the Holy Spirit.

I was once at an afternoon meeting. The Lord had been graciously with us and many had been healed by the power of God. Most of the people had gone home and I was left alone; then I saw a young man who was evidently hanging back to have a word. I asked, "What do you want?" He said, "I wonder if I could ask you to pray for me." I said, "What's the trouble?" He said, "Can't you smell?" The young fellow had gone into sin and was suffering the consequences. He said, "I have been turned out of two hospitals. I am broken out all over. I have abscesses all over me." And I could see that he had a bad breaking out at the nose. He said, "I heard you preach and could not understand about this healing business and was wondering if there was any hope for me."

I said to him, "Do you know Jesus?" He did not know the first thing about salvation, but I said to him, "Stand still." I placed my hands on his head and then on his loins and cursed that terrible disease in the name of Jesus. He cried out, "I know I'm healed. I can feel a warmth and a glow all over me." I said, "Who did it?" He said, "Your prayers." I said, "No, it was Jesus!" He said, "Was it He? O Jesus! Jesus! Jesus, save me." And that young man went away healed and saved. Oh, what a merciful God we have! What a wonderful Jesus is ours!

Are you oppressed? Cry out to God. It is always good for people to cry out. You may have to cry out. The Holy Spirit and the Word of God will bring to light every hidden, unclean thing that must be revealed. There is always a place of deliverance when you let God search out that which is spoiling and

marring your life. That evil spirit that was in the man
in the synagogue cried out, "Let us alone!" It was a
singular thing that the evil spirit had never cried out
like that until Jesus walked into the place where he
was. Jesus rebuked the thing, saying, "Hold thy peace
and come out of him," and the man was delivered. He
is just the same Jesus, exposing the powers of evil, delivering the captives and letting the oppressed go
free, purifying them and cleansing their hearts. Those
evil spirits that inhabited the man who had the legion
did not want to be sent to the pit to be tormented before their time, and so they cried out to be sent into
the swine. Hell is such an awful place that even the
demons hate the thought of going there. How much
more should men seek to be saved from the pit?

God is compassionate and says, "Seek ye the Lord
while he may be found." And He has further stated,
"Whosoever shall call on the name of the Lord shall
be saved." Seek Him now, call on His name right
now. There is forgiveness, healing, redemption, deliverance, and everything you need right here and now,
and that which will satisfy you throughout eternity.

BLESSINGS IN AUSTRALIA

Sister Winnie Andrews, N. Melbourne, Australia,
writes: "Our Brother Wigglesworth landed here Feb-
ruary 16th, and had a meeting that very night. The
dear Lord was present and that to heal. A little girl of
six, having never walked, after she had been prayed
for, walked out of the front door with her mother,
who was full of joy for what the Lord had done for
her little one. Another man who had been suffering
with bad feet for years and walked only with the aid
of a stick was instantly healed and has been along

several times to testify to what the Lord has done for him. Many dear people have been delivered in answer to the prayer of faith. One night a dear man and his wife whom he brought to the meeting in a wheel chair, were both healed. He had been suffering from deafness for 20 years and she had not walked for over 6½ years. After prayer she got out of her chair and walked to the station with her husband pushing the empty chair. He, too, was rejoicing in that he was now able to hear perfectly. O what a wonderful God we have. Blessed be His holy Name!

"At the Sunday afternoon service, a dear young woman who had been suffering with tuberculosis for 13 years and who was in the last stages, came leaning on the arm of a friend and was prayed for. At once she received new life and was perfectly delivered. The terrible burning sores which were eating their way into her bones have dried up and are peeling off, and she is looking so well and happy and is as strong as can be. Glory to God! Last night a young man suffering from consumption was prayed for and was instantly made whole. O, our hearts overflow at the glorious things God is doing in our midst!

"Many have been healed of neuritis, heart and lung trouble and stiff joints. One woman who had not walked for 22 years and could not as much as turn her head—after prayer—got out of bed and walked. Praise God!"—*The Pentecostal Evangel*, April 15, 1922.

3

The Power of the Name

Scripture Reading, Acts 3:1-16

All things are possible through the name of Jesus. God hath highly exalted Him and given Him the name which is above every name, that at the name of Jesus every knee should bow. There is power to overcome everything in the world through the name of Jesus. I am looking forward to a wonderful union through the name of Jesus. There is none other name under heaven given among men, whereby we must be saved.

I want to instill into you a sense of the power, the virtue and the glory of that name. Six people went into the house of a sick man to pray for him. He was an Episcopalian vicar, and lay in his bed utterly helpless, without even strength to help himself. He had read a little tract about healing and had heard about people praying for the sick. So he sent for these friends, who, he thought, could pray the prayer of faith. He was anointed according to James 5:14, but because he had no immediate manifestation of healing, he wept bitterly. The six people walked out of the room, somewhat crestfallen to see the man lying there in an unchanged condition.

When they were outside, one of the six said, "There is one thing we might have done. I wish you would all go back with me and try it." They went back and all got together in a group. This brother said, "Let us whisper the name of Jesus." At first when they whispered this worthy name nothing seemed to happen. But as they continued to whisper, "Jesus! Jesus! Jesus!" the power began to fall. As they saw that God was beginning to work, their faith and joy increased, and they whispered the name louder and louder. As they did so the man arose from his bed and dressed himself. The secret was just this: those six people had gotten their eyes off the sick man, and they were just taken up with the Lord Jesus Himself, and their faith grasped the power that there is in His name. Oh, if people would only appreciate the power that there is in this name, there is no telling what would happen.

I know that through His name and through the power of His name we have access to God. The very face of Jesus fills the whole place with glory. All over the world there are people magnifying that name, and Oh, what a joy it is for me to utter it.

One day I went up a mountain to pray. I had a wonderful day. It was one of the high mountains of Wales. I heard of one man going up this mountain to pray, and the Spirit of the Lord met him so wonderfully that his face shone like that of an angel when he returned. Everyone in the village was talking about it. As I went up to this mountain and spent the day in the presence of the Lord, His wonderful power seemed to envelop and saturate me.

Two years before this time there had come to our house two lads from Wales. They were just ordinary lads, but they became very zealous for God. They came to our mission and saw some of the works of God. They said to me, "We would not be surprised if the Lord brings you down to Wales to raise our Lazarus." They explained that the leader of their assembly was a man who had spent his days working in a tin mine and his nights preaching, and the result was that he had collapsed, gone into consumption, and for four years he had been a helpless invalid, having to be fed with a spoon.

While I was on that mountain top I was reminded of the transfiguration scene, and I felt that the Lord's only purpose in taking us into the glory was to fit us for greater usefulness in the valley. The Lord said to me, "I want you to go and raise Lazarus." I told the brother who accompanied me of this; and when we got down to the valley, I wrote a postcard: "When I was up on the mountain praying today, God told me that I was to go and raise Lazarus." I addressed the postcard to the man in the place whose name had been given to me by the two lads.

When we arrived at the place we went to the man to whom I had addressed the card. He looked at me and said, "Did you send this?" I said, "Yes." He said, "Do you think we believe in this? Here, take it." And he threw it at me.

The man called a servant and said, "Take this man and show him Lazarus." Then he said to me, "The moment you see him you will be ready to go home. Nothing will hold you." Everything he said was true from the natural viewpoint. The man was helpless. He was nothing but a mass of bones with skin stretched over them. There was no life to be seen. Everything in him spoke of decay.

I said to him, "Will you shout? You remember that at Jericho the people shouted while the walls were still up. God has like victory for you if you will only believe." But I could not get him to believe. There was not an atom of faith there. He had made up his mind not to have anything.

It is a blessed thing to learn that God's word can never fail. Never harken to human plans. God can work mightily when you persist in believing Him in spite of discouragements from the human standpoint. When I got back to the man to whom I had sent the postcard, he asked, "Are you ready to go now?"

I am not moved by what I see. I am *moved only by what I believe.* No man looks at appearances if he believes. No man considers how he feels if he believes. The man who believes God has it. Every man who comes into the Pentecostal experience can laugh at all things and believe God. There is something in the Pentecostal work that is different from anything else in the world. Somehow in Pentecost you know that God is a reality. Wherever the Holy Spirit has right of way, the gifts of the Spirit will be in manifestation; and where these gifts are never in manifestation, I question whether He is present. Pentecostal people are not satisfied with non-Pentecostal meetings. We want none of the entertainment that some of the churches are offering. When God comes in He entertains us Himself. *Entertained by the King of kings and Lord of lords!*

There were difficult conditions in that Welsh village, and it seemed impossible to get the people to believe. "Ready to go home?" I was asked. But a man and a woman there asked us to come and stay with them. I said, "I want to know how many of you people can pray." No one wanted to pray. I asked if I could get seven people to pray with me for the poor man's deliverance. I said to the two people who were going to entertain us, "I will count on you two, and there is my friend and myself, and we need three others." I told the people that I trusted that some of them would awaken to their privilege and come in the morning and join us in prayer for the raising of Lazarus. It will never do to give way to human opinions. If God says a thing, you are to believe it.

I told the people that I would not eat anything that night. When I got to bed it seemed as if the devil tried to place on me everything that he had placed on that poor man in the bed. When I awoke I had a cough and all the weakness of a tubercular patient. I rolled out of bed on the floor and cried out to God to deliver me from the power of the devil. I shouted loud enough to wake everybody in the house, but nobody was disturbed. God gave victory, and I got back into bed again as free as ever I was in my life. At five o'clock the Lord awakened me and said to me, "Don't break bread until you break it round My table." At six o'clock He gave me these words, "And I will raise him up." I put my elbow into the fellow who was sleeping with me. He said "Ugh!" I put my elbow into him again and said, "Do you hear? The Lord says that He will raise him up."

At eight o'clock they said to me, "Have a little refreshment." But I have found prayer and fasting the greatest joy, and you will always find it so when you are led by God. When we went to the house where Lazarus lived there were eight of us altogether. No one can prove to me that God does not always answer prayer. He always does more than that. He always gives the exceedingly abundant above all we ask or think.

I shall never forget how the power of God fell on us as we went into that sick man's room. Oh, it was lovely! As we circled round the bed I got one brother to hold one of the sick man's hands and I held the other; and we each held the hand of the person next to us. I said, "We are not going to pray, we are just going to use the name of Jesus." We all knelt down

and whispered that one word, "Jesus! Jesus! Jesus!"
The power of God fell and then it lifted. Five times
the power of God fell and then it remained. But the
man in the bed was unmoved. Two years previous
someone had come along and had tried to raise him
up, and the devil had used his lack of success as a
means of discouraging Lazarus. I said, "I don't care
what the devil says; if God says he will raise you up,
it must be so. Forget everything else except what God
says about Jesus."

The sixth time the power fell and the sick man's
lips began moving and the tears began to fall. I said
to him, "The power of God is here; it is yours to accept." Then he made a confession: "I have been bitter
in my heart, and I know I have grieved the Spirit of
God. Here I am helpless. I cannot lift my hands, nor
even lift a spoon to my mouth." I said, "Repent, and
God will hear you." He repented and cried out, "O
God, let this be to Thy glory." As he said this the virtue of the Lord went right through him.

I have asked the Lord to never let me tell this story
except as it was, for I realize that God can not bless
exaggerations. As we again said, "Jesus! Jesus! Jesus!"
the bed shook, and the man shook. I said to the people that were with me, "You can all go down stairs
right away. This is all God. I'm not going to assist
him." I sat and watched that man get up and dress
himself. We sang the doxology as he walked down the
steps. I said to him, "Now tell what has happened."

It was soon noised abroad that Lazarus had been
raised up and the people came from Llanelly and all
the district round to see him and hear his testimony.
And God brought salvation to many. This man told in
the open-air meeting what God had done, and as a result many were convicted and converted. All this

came through the name of Jesus, through faith in His name, yea, the faith that is by Him gave this sick man perfect soundness in the presence of them all.

Peter and John were helpless, were illiterate, they had no college education. But they had been with Jesus. To them had come a wonderful revelation of the power of the name of Jesus. They had handed out the bread and fish after Jesus had multiplied them. They had sat at the table with Him and John had often gazed into His face. Peter had often been rebuked, but Jesus manifested His love to Peter through it all. Yea, He loved Peter, the wayward one. Oh, He's a wonderful lover! I have been wayward, I have been stubborn, I had an unmanageable temper at one time, but how patient He has been. I am here to tell you that there is power in Jesus and in His wondrous name to transform anyone, to heal anyone.

If you will see Him as God's Lamb, as God's beloved Son who had laid upon Him the iniquity of us all, if only you will see that Jesus paid the whole price for our redemption that we might be free, you can enter into your purchased inheritance of salvation, of life, and of power.

Poor Peter and poor John! They had no money! But they had faith; they had the power of the Holy Spirit; they had God. You can have God even though you have nothing else. Even though you have lost your character you can have God. I have seen the worst men saved by the power of God.

I was one day preaching about the name of Jesus, and there was a man leaning against a lamppost, listening. It took a lamppost to enable him to keep on his feet. We had finished our open-air meeting, and the man was still leaning against the post. I asked him, "Are you sick?" He showed me his hand and I

saw beneath his coat he had a silver-handled dagger.
He told me that he was on his way to kill his unfaith-
ful wife, but that he had heard me speaking about the
power of the name of Jesus and could not get away.
He said that he felt helpless. I said, "Get you down."
And there on the square, with people passing up and
down, he got saved.

I took him to my home and put on him a new suit. I
saw there was something in that man that God could
use. He said to me the next morning, "God has revealed Jesus to me; I see that all has been laid upon
Jesus." I loaned him some money, and he soon got together a wonderful little home. His faithless wife was
living with another man, but he invited her back to
the home that he had prepared for her. She came; and
where enmity and hatred had been before, the whole
situation was transformed by love. God made that
man a minister wherever he went. There is power in
the name of Jesus. God can save to the uttermost.

We had a meeting in Stockholm that I shall always
remember. There was a home for incurables there and
one of the patients was brought to the meeting. He had
palsy and was shaking all over. He stood up before
three thousand people and came to the platform, sup-
ported by two others. The power of God fell on him as
I anointed him in the name of Jesus. The moment I
touched him he dropped his crutch and began to walk
in the name of Jesus. He walked down the steps and
round that great building in view of all the people.
There is nothing that our God cannot do. He will do
everything if you will dare to believe.

Someone asked me, "Will you go to this home for
incurables?" They took me there on my rest day. They
brought out the sick people into a great corridor and
in one hour the Lord set about twenty of them free.

The name of Jesus is so marvelous. Peter and John had no conception of all that was in that name; neither had the man, lame from his mother's womb, who was laid daily at the gate; but they had faith to say, "In the name of Jesus Christ of Nazareth, rise up and walk." And as Peter took him by the right hand and lifted him up, immediately his feet and ankle bones received strength, and he went into the Temple with them, walking and leaping and praising God. God wants you to see more of this sort of thing done. How can it be done? Through His name, through faith in His name, through faith which is by Him.

REVIVALS IN SCANDINAVIA

By Anna Lewini in *Confidence*

The writer had the privilege for three months one year of being in the center of Mr. Smith Wigglesworth's meetings in both Sweden and Denmark. It was a time of visitation from on high. I dare to say that hundreds of people received Jesus as their Saviour, thousands were healed from all kinds of diseases; also thousands of believers awoke to a new life, and many, many received the baptism of the Holy Spirit as on the day of Pentecost. For all this we give glory to Jesus. Here are a few examples of miracles my eyes have seen.

In was in Orebro (Sweden) where at that time there was held a Pentecostal Convention. I came to seek help myself, being worn out with long, unbroken service in the Lord's work. The next day there was a meeting for healing. After the preaching service I went forward into the other hall and I was surprised to find in a few minutes a crowd following. The hall was soon filled with hundreds of men and women patiently waiting for a touch of God through His servant, and, glory to God, we were not disappointed. As hands were laid upon me the power of God went through me in a mighty way. I was immediately well.

It was wonderful to notice, as the ministry continued, the effect upon the people as the power of the Lord came over them. Some lifted their hands, crying, "I am healed! I am healed!" Some fell on the platform under the power of the Spirit, having to be helped down. Others walked away as in a dream; others as drunk with new wine, lost to everything but God; but all had faces as transfigured with the glory of the Lord and magnifying Jesus. A young blind girl, as she was ministered to, cried out, "Oh, how many windows there are in this hall!" During the three weeks the meeting continued the great chapel was crowded daily, multitudes being healed and many saved. The testimony meetings were wonderful. One said, "I was deaf, they prayed, and Jesus healed me." Another, "I had consumption, and I am free." And so on.

At Skofde, in the smaller hall set apart for those seeking the Baptism of the Holy Spirit, I shall never forget the sight, how the people with eyes closed and hearts uplifted to God waited. Did the Holy Spirit fall upon them? Of course He did. Here also many were healed. At another place there was a young man whose body was spoiled because of sin, but the Lord is merciful with sinners. He was anointed, and when hands were laid on him, the power of God went mightily over him. He said, "I am healed," but being broken down, he cried as a little child, confessing his sin; at the same moment the Lord saved him. Glory to

God! He went into the large hall and testified to salvation and healing.

At Stockholm, long lines of people waited for hours to get in. The hall held 1,800 people. At nearly every meeting crowds were unable to enter the building, but they waited on, often hours and hours, for the chance, if any left the building to step into the place. Here a man with two crutches, his whole body shaking with palsy, is lifted onto the platform. (Behind him five or six hundred more are waiting for help.) This man is anointed and hands laid upon him in the Name of Jesus. He is still shaking. Then he drops one crutch, and after a short time the other one. His body is still shaking, but he takes the first step out IN FAITH. Will it be? He lifts one foot and then the other, walks round the platform. The onlookers rejoice with him. Now he walks around the auditorium. Hallelujah!

During this meeting a woman began to shout and shout. The preacher told her to be quiet, but instead she jumped up on a chair, flourishing her arms about, and crying, "I am healed! I am healed! I had cancer in my mouth, and I was unsaved; but during the meeting, as I listened to the Word of God, the Lord has saved me and healed me of cancer in my mouth." She shouts again, "I am saved! I am saved! I am healed of cancer!" She was quite beside herself. The people laughed and cried together.

Here was another woman unable to walk, sitting on a chair as she was ministered to. Her experience was the same as hundreds of others. She rose up, looking around, wondering if after all it was a dream. Suddenly she laughed and said, "My leg is healed." Afterwards she said, "I am not saved," and streams of tears ran down her face. They prayed for her, and later she left the meeting healed and saved and full of joy. We have a wonderful Saviour; glory to His Holy Name!

Out of many many miracles in Norway, I quote two taken from Pastor Barratt's papers. "Korsets Seir" (the Victory of the Cross). A man and his son came in a taxi to the meeting. Both had crutches. The father had been in bed two years and was unable to put his leg to the ground. He was ministered to. He dropped both crutches, walking and praising God. When the son saw this he cried out, "Help me too," and after a little while the father and son, without crutches and without taxi, walked away from the hall together. That word again is manifested; the same Jesus, the wonder-working Jesus is just the same today.

Now Copenhagen, my homeland! During three weeks thousands daily attended the meetings. Each morning two or three hundred were ministered to for healing. Each evening the platform was surrounded. Again and again, as each throng retired another company came forward seeking salvation. Here many were baptized in the Holy Spirit. The testimony meetings were wonderful.

Now I will close with a vision a brother had who attended these meetings. He was lost in intercession for the hundreds of sick waiting to be ministered to for healing. He saw an opening from the platform, where the sick were, right into the glory. He saw wonderful beings in the form of men resting who, with interest, looked on. Again he looked at the platform and saw a heavenly Being clothed in white, who all the time was more active than any other in helping the sick, and when HE touched them the effect was wonderful. Bent forms were made straight, their eyes shone, they began to glorify and praise the Lord. A Voice said: "Healings are the smallest of the gifts; it is but a drop in the bucket in view of what God has in store for His children. Ye shall do greater works than these."

4

Wilt Thou Be Made Whole?

Scripture Reading, John 5:1-24

I believe the word of God is so powerful that it can transform any life. There is power in God's word to make that which does not appear to appear. There is executive power in the word that proceeds from His lips. The psalmist tells us, "He sent his word, and healed them" (Psalms 107:20). Do you think that word has diminished in its power? I tell you nay, but God's word can bring things to pass today as of old.

The psalmist said, "Before I was afflicted I went astray: but now have I kept thy word." And again, "It is good for me that I have been afflicted; that I might learn thy statutes" (Psalms 119:67, 71). And if our afflictions will bring us to the place where we see that we cannot live by bread alone, but must partake of every word that proceedeth out of the mouth of God, they will have served a blessed purpose. But I want you to realize there is a life of purity, a life made clean through the word He has spoken, in which, through faith, you can glorify God with a body that is free from sickness, as well as with a spirit set free from the bondage of Satan.

There they were, a great multitude of impotent folk, of blind, halt, withered, around the pool, waiting for the moving of the water. Did Jesus heal everybody? He left many around that pool unhealed. There were doubtless many who had their eyes on the pool and who had no eyes for Jesus. There are many today who have their confidence in things seen. If they would only get their eyes on God instead of on natural things, how quickly they would be helped.

The question arises, Is salvation and healing for all? It is for all who will press in and get their portion. You remember the case of that Syrophenician woman who wanted the devil cast out of her daughter. Jesus said to her, "Let the children first be filled: for it is not meet to take the children's bread, and to cast it unto the dogs." Note, healing and deliverance are here spoken of by the Master as "the children's bread"; so, if you are a child of God, you can surely press in for your portion.

The Syrophenician woman (Mark 7:24-30) purposed to get from the Lord what she was after, and she said, "Yes, Lord: yet the dogs under the table eat of the children's crumbs." Jesus was stirred as He saw the faith of this woman, and He told her, "For this saying go thy way; the devil is gone out of thy daughter." Today there are many children of God refusing their blood-purchased portion of health in Christ and are throwing it away, while sinners are pressing through and picking it up from under the table, as it were; and they are finding the cure not only for their bodies but for their spirits and souls as well. The Syrophenician woman went home and found that the devil had indeed gone out of her daughter. Today there is bread, there is life, there is health for every child of God through His all-powerful Word.

The Word can drive every disease away from your body. It is your portion in Christ, Him who is our bread, our life, our health, our all in all. And though

you may be deep in sin, you can come to Him in repentance, and He will forgive and cleanse and heal
you. His words are spirit and life to those who will receive them. There is a promise in the last verse in
Joel, "I will cleanse their blood that I have not
cleansed." This is as much as to say He will provide
new life within. The life of Jesus Christ, God's Son,
can so purify men's hearts and minds that they become entirely transformed, spirit, soul, and body.

There they are round the pool; and this man had
been there a long time. His infirmity was of thirty-
eight years standing. Now and again an opportunity
would come as the angel stirred the waters, but his
heart would be made sick as he saw another step in
and be healed before him. But one day Jesus was
passing that way, and seeing him lying there in that
sad condition, asked, "Wilt thou be made whole?"
Jesus said it, and His word is from everlasting to everlasting. This is His word to you, poor, tried and tested
one today. You may say, like this poor impotent man,
"I have missed every opportunity up till now." Never
mind about that—*Wilt thou be made whole?*

I visited a woman who had been suffering for many
years. She was all twisted with rheumatism and had
been two years in bed. I asked her, "What makes you
lie here?" She said, "I've come to the conclusion that I
have a thorn in the flesh." I said, "To what wonderful
degree of righteousness have you attained that you
have to have a thorn in the flesh? Have you had such
an abundance of divine revelations that there is
danger of your being exalted above measure?" She
said, "I believe it is the Lord who is causing me to
suffer." I said, "You believe it is the Lord's will for
you to suffer, and you are trying to get out of it as
quickly as you can. There are doctor's bottles all over

the place. Get out of your hiding-place and confess
that you are a sinner. If you'll get rid of your self-
righteousness, God will do something for you. Drop
the idea that you are so holy that God has got to af-
flict you. Sin is the cause of your sickness and not
righteousness. Disease is not caused by righteousness,
but by sin."

There is healing through the blood of Christ and
deliverance for every captive. God never intended His
children to live in misery because of some affliction
that comes directly from the devil. A perfect atonement was made at Calvary. I believe that Jesus bore
my sins, and I am free from them all. I am justified
from all things if I dare believe. He Himself took our
infirmities and bare our sicknesses; and if I dare believe, I can be healed.

See this poor, helpless man at the pool. "Wilt thou
be made whole?" But there is a difficulty in the way.
The man has one eye on the pool and one on Jesus.
There are many people getting cross-eyed this way
these days; they have one eye on the doctor and one
on Jesus. If you will only look to Christ and put both
your eyes on Him, you can be made every whit
whole, spirit, soul, and body. It is the word of the living God that they that believe should be justified,
made free from all things. And whom the Son sets
free is free indeed.

You say, "Oh, if I only could believe!" He under-
stands. Jesus *knew* the man by the pool had been a
long time in that condition. He is full of compassion.
He knows that kidney trouble, He knows those corns,
He knows that neuralgia. There is nothing He does
not know. He only wants a chance to show Himself
merciful and gracious to you. But He wants to encourage you to believe Him. If you can only believe,

you can be saved and healed. Dare to believe that Jesus was wounded for your transgressions, was bruised for your iniquities, was chastised that you might have peace, and that by His stripes there is healing for you right here and now. You have failed because you have not believed Him. Cry out to Him even now, "Lord, I believe, help Thou mine unbelief."

I was in Long Beach, California, one day, and with a friend was passing a hotel. He told me of a doctor there who had a diseased leg and that he had been suffering from it for six years and could not get out. We went up to his room and found four doctors there. I said, "Well, doctor, I see you have plenty here, I'll call again another day." I was passing at another time, and the Spirit said, "Go join thyself to him." Poor doctor! He surely was in a bad condition. He said, "I have been like this for six years, and nothing human can help me." I said, "You need God Almighty." People are trying to patch up their lives; but you cannot do anything without God. I talked to him for awhile about the Lord and then prayed for him. I cried, "Come out of him, in the name of Jesus." The doctor cried, "It's all gone!"

Oh, if we only knew Jesus! One touch of His mightiness meets the need of every crooked thing. We must get people to believe Him. The simplicity of this salvation is wonderful. One touch of living faith in Him is all that is required, and wholeness is your portion.

I was in Long Beach about six weeks later, and the sick were coming for prayer. Among those filling up the aisle was the doctor. I asked, "What is the trouble?" He answered, "Diabetes, but it will be all right tonight. I know it will be all right." There is no such thing as the Lord not meeting your need. There are no "if's" or "may's"; His promises are all "shall's." All things are possible to him that believeth. Oh, the name of Jesus! There is power in that name to meet every condition of human need.

At that meeting there was an old man helping his son to the altar. He said, "He has fits—many every day." Then there was a woman with a cancer. Oh, what sin has done! We read that, when God brought forth His people from Egypt, "there was not one feeble person among their tribes" (Psalms 105:37). No disease! All healed by the power of God! I believe that God wants a people like that today.

I prayed for the sister who had the cancer, and she said, "I know I'm free and that God has delivered me." Then they brought the boy with the fits, and I commanded the evil spirits to leave in the name of Jesus. Then I prayed for the doctor. At the next night's meeting the building was full. I called out, "Now, doctor, what about the diabetes?" He said, "It has gone." Then I said to the old man, "What about your son?" He said, "He hasn't had any fits since." We have a God who answers prayer.

Jesus meant this man at the pool to be a testimony forever. When he had both eyes on Jesus, He said to him, "Do the impossible thing. Rise, take up thy bed, and walk." Jesus called on the man with the withered hand to do the impossible—to stretch forth his hand. The man did the impossible thing—he stretched out his hand, and it was made whole. And so with this impotent man—he began to rise, and he found the power of God moving within. He wrapped up his bed and began to walk off. It was the sabbath day, and there were some of those folks around who think much more of a day than they do of the Lord; and they began to make a fuss. When the power of God is being demonstrated, a protest will always come from

hypocrites. Jesus knew all about what the man was
going through and met him again; and this time He
said to him, "Behold, thou art made whole: sin no
more, lest a worse thing come unto thee."

There is a close relationship between sin and sickness. How many know that their sickness is a direct
result of sin? I hope that no one will ask to be prayed
for who is living in sin. But if you will obey God and
repent of your sin and quit it, God will meet you, and
neither your sickness nor your sin will remain. "The
prayer of faith shall save the sick, and the Lord shall
raise him up; and if he have committed sins, they
shall be forgiven him" (James 5:15).

Faith is the open door through which the Lord
comes. Do not say, "I was healed by faith." Faith does
not save. God saves through that open door. Healing
comes the same way. You believe, and the virtue of
Christ comes. Healing is for the glory of God. I am
here because God healed me when I was dying; and I
have been all round the world preaching this full redemption, doing all I can to bring glory to the wonderful name of Jesus, through whom I was healed.

"Sin no more, lest a worse thing come upon thee."
The Lord told us in one place about an evil spirit
going out from a man. The house that he left was
then swept and garnished, but it received no new oc-
cupant. And that evil spirit, with seven other spirits
more wicked than himself, went back to that unoccu-
pied house, and the last stage of the man was worse
than the first. The Lord heals you for His glory and
that from henceforth your life shall glorify Him. But
this man remained stationary. He did not magnify
God. He did not seek to be filled with the Spirit. And
his last state became worse than the first.

The Lord would so cleanse the motive and desires

of our hearts that we will seek but one thing only: His glory. I went to a certain place one day and the Lord said, "This is for My glory." A young man had been sick for a long time confined to his bed in an utterly hopeless condition. He was fed only with a spoon and was never dressed. The weather was damp, and so I said to the people of the house, "I wish you would put the young man's clothes by the fire to air." At first they would not take any notice of my request; but because I was persistent, they at last got out his clothes, and, when they were aired, I took them into his room.

The Lord said to me, "You will have nothing to do with this"; and I just lay out prostrate on the floor. The Lord showed me that He was going to shake the place with His glory. The very bed shook. I laid my hands on the young man in the name of Jesus, and the power fell in such a way that I fell with my face to the floor. In about a quarter of an hour the young man got up and walked up and down praising God. He dressed himself and then went out to the room where his father and mother were. He said, "God has healed me." Both the father and mother fell prostrate to the floor as the power of God surged through that room. There was a woman in that house who had been in an asylum for lunacy, and her condition was so bad that they were about to take her back. But the power of God healed her, too. The power of God is just the same today as of old. Men need to be taken back to the old paths, to the old-time faith, to believe God's Word and every "Thus saith the Lord" therein. The Spirit of the Lord is moving in these days. God is coming forth. If you want to be in the rising tide, you must accept all God has said.

"Wilt thou be made whole?" It is Jesus who asks it.

Give Him your answer. He will hear and He will answer.

BLESSINGS IN AUSTRALIA

The following is from Melbourne, Australia, from Sister Winnie Andrews, in connection with Brother Wigglesworth's ministry there:

A young woman declares: "I was brought to last Sunday's meeting a poor, dying woman, with a disease which was eating into every part of my being. I was full of corruption outside as well as in; but the Lord Jesus Christ came and loosed me and set me free. Since then I have slept better and have eaten more heartily than I have for eight years."

The president of the Methodist Local Preachers' Association testified to having been delivered from nervous trouble.

Mr. Solglush, a prominent business man, testified to deliverance from an affliction in the feet since he was two years old; now he is fifty-two. "Since I was prayed for in the name of Jesus all pain is gone. No one has ever seen me do this (stamping his feet). I have no use for my stick."

A lady said: "While sitting in my seat, listening to the Word, God healed me of liver trouble, gall stones, and sciatica. He has also touched my daughter who was suffering with her feet, having been operated on twice; she had little hope of being anything but an invalid; but the Lord operated. All pain has gone. Praise the Lord."

Mr. Lewellyn, a Church of England reader, testified to having been immediately healed of a stiff knee.

Mr. Barrett testified that Miss Witt, of Box Hill, who has been 22 years in an invalid chair, rose and walked after Mr. Wigglesworth ministered unto her in the name of Jesus.

Another testified of having been healed the night before of rheumatoid arthritis of four years standing, discarding crutch and stick.

Mr. Johnsone of Sperm Vale, who had been deaf twenty years, and his wife, who had sat in a wheelchair for six years, were immediately healed. The empty chair was wheeled to the railway station, the woman testifying to passersby of the great things God had done for her.

Many were healed through the application of handkerchiefs.—From *The Pentecostal Evangel.*

5

I Am the Lord That Healeth Thee

"Is any sick among you? Let him call for the elders of the church; and let them pray over him, anointing him with oil in the name of the Lord: and the prayer of faith shall save the sick, and the Lord shall raise him up; and if he have committed sins, they shall be forgiven him" (James 5:14, 15).

We have in this precious word a real basis for the truth of healing. In this passage God gives very definite instructions to the sick. If you are sick, your part is to call for the elders of the church; it is their part to anoint and pray for you in faith, and then the whole situation rests with the Lord. When you have been anointed and prayed for, you can rest assured that the Lord will raise you up. It is the word of God.

I believe that we all can see that the church cannot play with this business. If any turn away from these clear instructions they are in a place of tremendous danger. Those who refuse to obey, do so to their unspeakable loss.

James tells us in connection with this, "If any of you do err from the truth, and one convert him, let him know, that he which converteth the sinner from the error of his way shall save a soul from death." Many turn away from the Lord as did King Asa who sought the physicians in his sickness and consequently died; and I take it that this passage means that if one induces another to turn back to the Lord, he will save

such from death and God will forgive a multitude of
sins that they have committed. This verse can also
have a large application on the line of salvation. If
you turn away from any part of God's truth, the
enemy will certainly get an advantage over you.

Does the Lord meet those who look to Him for
healing and obey the instructions set forth in James?
Most assuredly. Let me tell you a story to show how
He will undertake for the most extreme case.

One day I had been visiting the sick, and was with
a friend of mine, an architect, when I saw a young
man from his office coming down the road in a car,
and holding in his hand a telegram. It contained a
very urgent request that we go immediately to pray
for a man who was dying. We went off in an auto as
fast as possible and in about an hour and a half
reached a large house in the country where the man
who was dying resided. There were two staircases in
that house, and it was extremely convenient; for the
doctors could go up and down one, and my friend
and I could go up and down the other, and so we had
no occasion to meet.

I learned that the man's body had been broken, he
was ruptured, and his bowels had been punctured in
two places. The discharge from the bowels had
formed abscesses, and blood poisoning had set in. The
man's face had turned green. Two doctors were working on the case, but they saw that it was beyond their
power. They had telegraphed to London for a great
specialist, and when we arrived they were at the railway station awaiting his arrival.

The man was very near death and could not speak.
I said to his wife, "If you desire, we will anoint and
pray for him." She said, "That is why I sent for you." I
anointed him in the name of the Lord and asked the

Lord to raise him up. Apparently there was no change. (God often hides what He does. From day to day we find that **God** is doing wonderful things, and we receive reports of healings that have taken place that we heard nothing about at the time of our meetings. Only last night a woman came into the meeting suffering terribly. Her whole arm was filled with poison, and her blood was so poisoned that it was certain to bring her to her death. We rebuked the thing, and she was here this morning and told us that she was without pain and had slept all night, something she had not done for two months. To God be all the praise. You will find He will do this kind of thing all along.)

As soon as we anointed and prayed for this brother we went down the back staircase and the three doctors came up the front staircase. As we arrived downstairs, I said to my friend who had come with me, "Friend let me have hold of your hands." We held each other's hands, and I said to him, "Look into my face and let us agree together, according to Matthew 18:19, that this man shall be brought out of this death." We laid the whole matter before God, and said, "Father, we believe."

Then the conflict began. The wife came down to us and said, "The doctors have all their instruments out and they are about to operate." I cried, "What? Look here, he's your husband, and I tell you this, if those men operate on him, he will die. Go back and tell them you cannot allow it." She went back to the doctors and said, "Give me ten minutes." They said, "We can't afford to, the man is dying and it is your husband's only chance." She said, "I want ten minutes, and you don't touch his body until I have them."

They went downstairs by one staircase and we

went up by the other. I said to the woman, "This man is your husband, and he cannot speak for himself. It is now the time for you to put your whole trust in God and prove Him wholly true. You can save him from a thousand doctors. You must stand with God and for God in this critical hour." After that, we came down and the doctors went up. The wife faced those three doctors and said, "You shan't touch this man's body. He is my husband. I am sure that if you operate on him he will die, but he will live if you don't touch him."

Suddenly the man in the bed spoke. "God has done it," he said. They rolled back the bed clothes and the doctors examined him, and the abscesses were cut clear away. The nurse cleaned the place where they had been. The doctors could see the bowels still open and they said to the wife, "We know that you have great faith, and we can see that a miracle has taken place. But you must let us untie these broken parts and put in silver tubes, and we know that your husband will be all right after that, and it need not interfere with your faith at all." She said to them, "God has done the first thing and He can do the rest. No man shall touch him now." And God healed the whole thing. And that man is well and strong today.

Do you ask by what power this was done? I would answer in the words of Peter, "His name, *through faith in His name, made this man strong.*" The anointing was done *in the name of the Lord.* And it is written, *"The LORD shall raise him up."* And He provides the double cure; even if sin has been the cause of the sickness, His Word declares, "If he have committed sins, they shall be forgiven."

You ask, "What is faith?" Faith is the principle of the Word of God. The Holy Spirit, who inspired the

Word, is called the Spirit of Truth. As we receive with meekness the engrafted Word, faith springs in our heart—faith in the sacrifice of Calvary, faith in the shed blood of Jesus, faith in the fact that He took our weakness upon Himself, has borne our sicknesses and carried our pains, and that He is our life today.

God has chosen us to help one another. We dare not be independent. He brings us to a place where we submit ourselves to one another. If we refuse to do this, we get away from the Word of God and out of the place of faith. I have been in this place once and I trust I shall never be there again. I went one time to a meeting. I was very, very sick, and I got worse and worse. I knew the perfect will of God was for me to humble myself and ask the elders to pray for me. I put it off and the meeting finished. I went home without being anointed and prayed with, and everyone in the house caught the thing I was suffering with.

My boys did not know anything else but to trust the Lord as the family Physician, and my youngest boy, George, cried out from the attic, "Dadda, come." I cried, "I cannot come. The whole thing is from me. I shall have to repent and ask the Lord to forgive me." I made up my mind to humble myself before the whole church. Then I rushed to the attic and laid my hands on my boy in the name of Jesus. I placed my hands on his head and the pain left and went lower down; he cried again, "Put your hands still lower." At last the pain went right down to the feet and as I placed my hand on the feet he was completely delivered. Some evil power had evidently gotten hold and as I laid my hands on the different parts of the body it left. (We have to see the difference between anointing the sick and casting out demons.) God will always be gracious when we humble ourselves before Him and come to a place of brokenness of spirit.

I was in Havre in France and the power of God was being mightily manifested. A Greek named Felix attended the meeting and became very zealous for God. He was very anxious to get all the Catholics he could to the meeting so they should see that God was graciously visiting France. He found a certain bed-ridden woman who was fixed in a certain position and could not move, and he told her about the Lord healing at the meetings and that he would get me to come if she wished. She said, "My husband is a Catholic and he would never allow anyone who was not a Catholic to see me."

She asked her husband to allow me to come and told him what Felix had told her about the power of God working in our midst. He said, "I will have no Protestant enter my house." She said, "You know the doctors cannot help me, and the priests cannot help, won't you let this man of God pray for me?" He finally consented and I went to the house. The simplicity of this woman and her child-like faith were beautiful to see.

I showed her my oil bottle and said to her, "Here is oil. It is a symbol of the Holy Spirit. When that comes upon you, the Holy Spirit will begin to work, and the Lord will raise you up." And God did something the moment the oil fell upon her. I looked toward the window and I saw Jesus. (I have seen Him often. There is no painting that is like Him: no artist can ever depict the beauty of my lovely Lord.) The woman felt the power of God in her body and cried, "I'm free, my hands are free, my shoulders are free, and oh, I see Jesus! I'm free! I'm free!"

The vision vanished and the woman sat up in bed. I

looked and saw the Lord again. She saw Him too and cried, "He's there again. I'm free! I'm free!" She rose from her bed and walked round the room praising God, and we were all in tears as we saw His wonderful works. The Lord shall raise them up when conditions are met.

When I was a young man I always loved the fellowship of elderly men and was always careful to hear what they had to say. I had a friend, an old Baptist minister who was a wonderful preacher. I spent much of my time with him. One day he came to me and said, "My wife is dying." I said, "Brother Clark, why don't you believe God? God can raise her up if you will only believe Him." He asked me to come to his house, and I looked for someone to go with me.

I went to a certain rich man who was very zealous for God and spent much money in opening up rescue missions, and I asked him to go with me. He said, "Never you mind me. You go yourself, but I don't take to this kind of business." Then I thought of a man who could pray by the hour, Brother Nichols. When he was on his knees he could go round the world three times and come out at the same place. I asked him to go with me and said to him, "You'll have a real chance this time. Keep at it, and quit when you're through." (Some go on after they are through.)

Brother Nichols went with me and started praying. He asked the Lord to comfort the husband in his great bereavement and prayed for the orphans and a lot more on this line. I cried, "O my God, stop this man." But there was no stopping him and he went on praying and there was not a particle of faith in anything he uttered. He did stop at last, and I said, "Brother Clark, it's now your turn to pray." He started, "Lord, answer the prayer of my brother and comfort me in this great bereavement and sorrow. Prepare me to face this great trial." I cried out, "My God, stop this man." The whole atmosphere was being charged with unbelief.

I had a glass bottle full of oil and I went up to the woman and poured the whole lot on her in the name of Jesus. Suddenly Jesus appeared. standing at the foot of the bed. He smiled and vanished. The woman stood up, perfectly healed, and she is a strong woman today.

We have a big God. We have a wonderful Jesus. We have a glorious Comforter. God's canopy is over you and will cover you at all times, preserving you from evil. Under His wings shalt thou trust. The Word of God is living and powerful and in its treasures you will find eternal life If you dare trust this wonderful Lord, this Lord of life. you will find in Him everything you need. You will find that if you dare trust Him, He will never fail. "The prayer of faith shall save the sick, and the LORD shall raise him up." Do you trust Him? He is worthy to be trusted.

I was one time asked to go to Weston-super-mare, a seaside resort in the West of England. I learned from a telegram that a man had lost his reason and had become a raving maniac, and they wanted me to pray for him. I arrived at the place, and the wife said to me, "Will you sleep with my husband?" I agreed, and in the middle of the night an evil power laid hold of him. It was awful. I put my hand on his head and his hair was like a lot of sticks. God gave deliverance—a temporary deliverance. At six o'clock the next morning, I felt that it was necessary that I should get out of the house for a short time.

The man saw me going and cried out, "If you leave

me, there is no hope." But I felt that I had to go. As I
went out I saw a woman with a Salvation Army bon-
net on and I knew that she was going to their seven
o'clock prayer meeting. And that is where I found myself a few minutes later. When I saw that the Captain
in charge was about to select a hymn. I spoke up,
"Captain, don't sing. Let's get to prayer." He agreed,
and I prayed my heart out, and then I grabbed my
hat and rushed out of the hall. They all thought they
had a madman in their prayer meeting that morning.

As I hurried toward the house where I had spent
the night, I saw the sick man rushing down toward
the sea without a stitch of clothing on. He was about
to drown himself. I cried, "In the name of Jesus, come
out of him!" The man fell full length on the ground
and that evil power went out of him never to return.
His wife came rushing after him, and the husband
was restored to her in a perfect mental condition.

There are evil powers, but Jesus is greater than all
evil powers. There are awful diseases, but Jesus is
healer. There is no case too hard for Him. The Lion
of Judah shall break every chain. He came to relieve
the oppressed and to set the captive free. He came to
bring redemption.

People want to know how to be kept by the
power of God. Every position of grace into which you
are led—forgiveness, healing, deliverance of any kind
—will be contested by Satan. He will contend for
your body. When you are saved, Satan will come
round and say, "See, you are not saved." The devil is
a liar. If he says you are not saved, it is a sure sign
that you are.

You will remember the story of the man who was
swept and garnished. The evil power had been swept
out of him. But the man remained in a stationary po-

sition. If the Lord heals you, you dare not remain in a stationary position. The evil spirit came back to that man and found the house swept, and took seven others worse than himself, and the last state of that man was worse than the first. Be sure to get filled with God. Get the Occupier. Be filled with the Spirit.

God has a million ways of undertaking for those who go to Him for help. He has deliverance for every captive. He loves you so much that He even says, "Before they call, I will answer." Don't turn Him away.

A TESTIMONY OF HEALING

"I slipped and fell, and as was afterwards discovered, fractured the coccyx (the base of the spine), and so severely wrenched the hips and pelvic bones that I became a great sufferer. As the broken bone was not discovered and set until about two months after the accident, the constant pain and irritation caused a general inflammation of the nervous system, and the long delay in getting the bone set made it impossible to heal. My condition steadily grew worse, and I was taken to the hospital and the bone was removed about a month after it had been set. Though the wound healed rapidly, the nervous inflammation remained, and so for many months longer I was in constant pain and unable to get around without assistance. I was taken to the first service held by Mr. Wigglesworth on the 2nd of October, 1922. At the close of the service all those who were sick and in pain and had come for healing were requested to rise if possible. My husband assisted me to my feet, and as those were prayed for by the speaker, I was instantly healed. How, I do not know. I only know the Great Physician touched my body and I was made whole, and freed from pain.

"After I got home I showed how I could sit down and rise with my hands above my head; when before it had taken both hands to push up my feeble body, and I had to have straps on my bed to pull up by. No more use for them now! I lay down and turned over for the first time without pain. I shall never cease to praise God for the healing of my body through the precious blood of Jesus and in His name. I walked to the street car alone the next day and attended the next service and have been on the go ever since. To Jesus be all the praise and glory."

—Mrs. Sanders,
San Diego, Calif.

6

Himself Took Our Infirmities

Scripture Reading, Matthew 8:1-17.

Here we have a wonderful word. All the Word is wonderful. This blessed Book brings such life and health and peace and such an abundance that we should never be poor. This Book is my heavenly bank. I find everything I want in it. I want to show you how rich you may be, that in everything you can be enriched in Christ Jesus. He has abundance of grace for you and the gift of righteousness, and through His abundant grace all things are possible. I want to show you that you can be a living branch of the living Vine, Christ Jesus, and that it is your privilege to be right here in this world what He is. John tells us, "As He is, so are we in this world." Not that we are anything in ourselves, but Christ within us is our all in all.

The Lord Jesus is always wanting to show forth His grace and love in order to draw us to Himself. God is willing to do things, to manifest His Word, and let us know in measure the mind of our God in this day and hour. There are many needy ones, many afflicted ones, but I do not think any are half as bad as this first case that we read of in Matthew 8. This man was a leper. You may be suffering with consumption or cancer or other things, but God will show forth His perfect cleansing, His perfect healing, if you have a living faith in Christ. He is a wonderful Jesus.

61

This leper must have been told about Jesus. How much is missed because people are not constantly telling what Jesus will do in our day. Probably someone had come to that leper and said, "Jesus can heal you." And so he was filled with expectation as he saw the Lord coming down the mountain side. Lepers were not allowed to come within reach of people; they were shut out as unclean. And so in the ordinary way it would have been very difficult for him to get near because of the crowd that surrounded Jesus. But as Jesus came down from the mount He met this poor leper. Oh, this terrible disease! There was no help for him, humanly speaking, but nothing is too hard for Jesus. The man cried, "Lord, if thou wilt, thou canst make me clean." Was Jesus willing? You will never find Jesus missing an opportunity of doing good. You will find that He is always more willing to work than we are to give Him an opportunity to work. The trouble is we do not come to Him, we do not ask Him for what He is more than willing to give.

And Jesus put forth His hand and touched him, saying, "I will; be thou clean." And immediately his leprosy was cleansed. I like that. If you are definite with Him, you will never go away disappointed. The divine life will flow into you and instantaneously you will be delivered. This Jesus is just the same today, and He says to you, "I will; be thou clean." He has an overflowing cup for you, a fullness of life. He will meet you in your absolute helplessness. All things are possible if you will only believe. God has a real plan. It is so simple. Just come to Jesus. You will find Him just the same as He was in days of old.

The second case in Matthew 8 is that of the centurion coming and beseeching Jesus on behalf of his servant who was sick of the palsy and grievously tormented. This man was so in earnest that he came seeking for Jesus. There is one thing certain: there is no such thing as seeking without finding. He that seeketh findeth. Listen to the gracious words of Jesus, "I will come and heal him." In most places that we go to there are so many people that we cannot pray for. In some places there are 200 or 300 who would like us to visit them, but we are not able to do so. But I am so glad that the Lord Jesus is always willing to come and heal. He longs to meet the sick ones. He loves to heal them of their afflictions. The Lord is healing many people today by means of handkerchiefs just as He healed people in the days of Paul. You can read of this in Acts 19:12.

A woman came to me in the city of Liverpool and said, "I would like you to help me. I wish you would join with me in prayer. My husband is a drunkard and every night comes into the home under the influence of drink. Won't you join me in prayer for him?" I said to the woman, "Have you a handkerchief?" She took out a handkerchief and I prayed over it and told her to lay it on the pillow of the drunken man. He came home that night and laid his head on the pillow in which this handkerchief was tucked. He laid his head on more than the pillow that night. He laid his head on the promise of God. In Mark 11:24, we read, "What things soever ye desire when ye pray, believe that ye receive them, and ye shall have them."

The next morning the man got up and stopped at the first saloon that he had to pass on his way to work and ordered some beer. He tasted it and said to the bartender, "You have put some poison in this beer." He could not drink it and went on to the next saloon and ordered some more beer. He tasted it and said to the man behind the counter, "You put some poison in this beer; I believe you folks have agreed to poison me." The bartender was indignant. The man said, "I will go somewhere else." He went to another saloon and the same thing happened as in the two previous saloons. He made such a fuss that they turned him out. After he got off work he went to another saloon to get some beer, and again he thought he had been poisoned; he made so much disturbance that he was thrown out. He went to his home and told his wife what had happened and said, "It seems as though all the fellows have agreed to poison me." His wife said to him, "Can't you see the hand of the Lord in this, that He is making you dislike the stuff that has been your ruin?" This word brought conviction to the man's heart, and he came to the meeting and got saved. The Lord has power to set the captives free.

When I was in Australia a lady came to me who was much troubled about her son who was so lazy. I prayed over a handkerchief which was placed on the boy's pillow. He slept that night on the handkerchief and the next morning he got up and went out and secured a position and went to work. Oh, praise the Lord! You can't shut God out, but if you will only believe He will shut the devil out.

Jesus was willing to go and heal the sick one but the centurion said, "Lord, I am not worthy that thou shouldest come under my roof: but speak the word only, and my servant shall be healed." Jesus was delighted with this expression and said to the man, "Go thy way; and as thou hast believed, so be it done unto thee." And this servant was healed the self-same hour.

When I was in Australia a man who was leaning on a big stick came up to me and said, "I would like you to help me. It will take you half an hour to pray for me." I said, "Believe God and in one moment you will be whole." His faith was quickened to receive an immediate healing and he went away glorifying God for a miraculous healing. The word of the Lord is sufficient today. If you will dare to believe God's Word, you will see a performance of His Word that will be truly wonderful. Here we have with the centurion an audacity of faith, a faith that did not limit God. Failures come when we limit the Holy One of Israel. I want to encourage you to a living faith to believe God's Word.

The next healing we read of in Matthew 8 is the healing of Peter's wife's mother who was sick of a fever. Luke tells us that Jesus rebuked the fever. The fever could hear. The moment it could hear it went. Jesus had a new method. Today there are a lot of folks who try to sweat out a fever. You can't sweat the devil out. He can stand all the heat that you can apply to him. But if you can believe, deliverance is as sure and certain for you as it was for Peter's wife's mother.

I received a telegram once urging me to visit a young woman about 200 miles from my home. As I went to this place I met the father and mother and found them brokenhearted. They led me up a staircase to a room where I saw a young woman on the floor and five people holding her down. She was a frail young woman, but the power in her was greater than all those young men. As I went into the room the evil powers looked out of her eyes and they used her lips saying, "We are many, you can't cast us out." I said, "Jesus can." He is equal to every occasion. He is waiting for an opportunity to bless. He is ready for every opportunity to deliver souls. When we receive Jesus it is true of us, "Greater is He that is in you than he that is in the world." He is greater than all the powers of darkness. No man can meet the devil in his own strength, but any man filled with the knowledge of Jesus, filled with His presence, filled with His power, is more than a match for the powers of darkness. God has called us to be more than conquerors through Him that loved us.

The living Word is able to destroy Satanic forces. There is power in the name of Jesus. I would that every window in the street displayed the name of Jesus. His name, through faith in His name, brought deliverance to this poor, bound soul, and thirty-seven demons came out giving their names as they came forth. The dear woman was completely delivered and they were able to give her back her child. That night there was heaven in that home and the father and mother and son and his wife were all united in glorifying Christ for His infinite grace. The next morning we had a gracious time in the breaking of bread. All things are wonderful with our wonderful Jesus. If you would dare rest your all upon Him, things would take place and He would change the whole situation. In a moment, through the name of Jesus, a new order of things can be brought in.

In the world they are always having new diseases and the doctors cannot locate them. A doctor said to me, "The science of medicine is in its infancy, and really we doctors have no confidence in our medicine. We are always experimenting." But the man of God does not experiment. He knows, or ought to know, the mightiness of the Lord Jesus Christ. He is not, or should not be, moved by outward observation but should get divine revelation of the mightiness of the name of Jesus and the power of His blood. If we exercise our faith in the Lord Jesus Christ, He will come forth and get glory over all the powers of darkness.

In the evening they brought unto Him many that were possessed with devils; and He cast out the spirits with His word and healed all that were sick: that it might be fulfilled which was spoken by Esaias the prophet, saying, "Himself took our infirmities, and bare our sicknesses." If you can only see the Lamb of God as He went to Calvary! He took our flesh that He might take upon Himself the full burden of all our sin and all the consequences of sin. There on the cross God laid upon Him the iniquities of us all. There on the cross of Calvary the results of sin were also dealt with. "As the children are partakers of flesh and blood, he also himself took part of the same; that through death he might destroy him that had the power of death, that is, the devil; and deliver them who through fear of death were all their lifetime subject to bondage" (Hebrews 2:14). Through His death there is deliverance for you today.

HUSBAND HEALED OF DOUBLE RUPTURE AND OTHER ILLS

My husband was instantly healed of double rupture of three years' standing, dropsy (two years), a weak heart, and tobacco chewing (forty-seven years), and praise the Lord, it was *all* taken away when the shock from heaven's battery went through him. It happened when we went to Portland, Oregon, to hear Brother Smith Wigglesworth. My husband was also healed instantly of heavy blood pressure and varicose veins. The veins had broken in his ankles and for a year had to be dressed twice a day. No doctor could help him, but, praise God, Jesus was the doctor and healed him.

Mrs. Frank Nephews

7

Our Risen Christ

Today we praise God for the fact that our glorious Jesus is the risen Christ. Those of us who have tasted the power of the indwelling Spirit know something of the manner in which the hearts of those two disciples burned as they walked to Emmaus with the risen Lord as their companion.

Note the words of Acts 4:31, "And when they had prayed, the place was shaken." There are many churches where they never pray the kind of prayer that you read of here. A church that does not know how to pray and to shout will never be shaken. If you attend a place like that you may as well write "Ichabod—the glory of the Lord has departed," over the threshold. It is only when men have learned the secret of prayer, of power, and of praise, that God comes forth. Some people say, "Well, I praise God inwardly," but if there is an abundance of praise in your heart, your mouth cannot help speaking it.

There was a man who had a large business in London who was a great church-goer. The church he attended was beautifully decorated, and his pew was delightfully cushioned—just about enough to make it easy to sleep through the sermons. He was a prosperous man in business, but he had no peace in his heart. But there was a boy at his business who always

68

looked happy. He was always jumping and whistling. One day the man said to this boy, "I want to see you in my office." When the boy was in his office he asked him, "How is it that you can always whistle and be happy?" "I cannot help it," answered the boy. "Where did you get it?" asked the man. "I got it at the Pentecostal mission." "Where is that?" The boy told him, and soon the man was attending services. The Lord broke him up there, and in a short while he was entirely changed. One day, shortly after this, he found instead of being distracted by his business as he formerly had been, he was actually whistling and jumping. His whole position and his whole life had been changed.

The shout cannot come out unless it is in. There must first be the inner working of the power of God. It is He who changes the heart and transforms the life; and before there is any real outward evidence there must be the inflow of divine life. Sometimes I say to people, "You weren't at meeting the other night." The reply, "Oh, yes, I was there in spirit." I say to them, "Well, come next time with your body also. We don't want a lot of spirits here and no bodies. We want you to come and get filled with God." When all the people will come and pray and praise as did these early disciples there will be something doing. People who come will catch fire and they will want to come again. But they will have no use for a place where everything has become formal, dry, and dead.

The power of Pentecost as it came at first came to loose men. God wants us free on every line. Men and women are tired of imitations; they want reality; they want to see people who have the living Christ within and are filled with Holy Ghost power.

I received several letters and telegrams about a sick young man, but when I arrived I was told I was too late. I said, "That cannot be. God has never sent me too late anywhere." God showed me when I went that something different would happen to anything I had seen previously. The people I went to were all strangers. I was introduced to a young man who lay helpless and for whom there was no hope. The doctor had been to see him that morning and had declared that he would not live through the day. He lay with his face to the wall, and when I spoke to him he whispered, "I cannot turn over." His mother said that they had had to lift him out of bed on sheets for weeks and that he was so weak and helpless that he had to stay in one position.

The young man said, "My heart is very weak." I assured him, "God is the strength of thy heart and thy portion forever. If you will believe God, it shall be so today."

Our Christ is risen. He is a living Christ who indwells us. We must not have this truth merely as a theory; Christ must be risen in us by the power of the Spirit. The power that raised Him from the dead must animate us; and as this glorious resurrection power surges through your being, you will be freed from all your weaknesses and you will become strong in the Lord and in the power of His might. There is a resurrection power that God wants you to have and to have it today. Why not? Receive your portion here and now.

I said to these people, "I believe your son will rise today." They only laughed. People do not expect to see signs and wonders today as the disciples saw them of old. Has God changed?, or has our faith waned so that we are not expecting the greater works that Jesus promised? We must not harp on any minor key. Our message must rise to concert pitch, and there must be nothing left out of it that is in the Book.

It was winter time, and I said to the parents, "Will you get the boy's suit and bring it here?" They would not listen to the request, for they were expecting the boy to die. But I had gone to that place believing God. In Romans 4:17 we read of Abraham: "(I have made thee a father of many nations,) before him whom he believed, even God, who quickeneth the dead, and calleth those things which be not as though they were." God help us to understand this. It is time people knew how to shout in faith as they contemplate the eternal power of our God to whom it is nothing to quicken and raise the dead. I come across some who would be giants in the power of God, but they have no shout of faith. I find everywhere people who fail, even when they are praying, simply because they are just breathing sentences without uttering speech; and you cannot get victory that way. You must learn to take the victory and shout in the face of the devil, "It is done!" There is no man who can doubt if he learns to shout. Things will be different, and tremendous things will happen. In verse 24 we read, "They lifted up their voice to God with one accord." It surely must have been a loud prayer. We must know that God means us to have life. If there is anything in the world that has life in it, it is this Pentecostal revival we are in. I believe in the baptism of the Holy Spirit with the speaking in tongues, and I believe that every man who is baptized in the Holy Spirit will speak in other tongues as the Spirit gives him utterance. I believe in the Holy Spirit. And if you are filled with the Spirit, you will be superabounding in life—living waters will flow from you.

At last I persuaded the parents to bring the boy's clothes and laid them on the bed. From the natural viewpoint, the young man lay dying. I spoke to the afflicted one, "God has revealed to me that, as I lay my hands upon you, the place will be filled with the Holy Spirit, the bed will be shaken, you will be shaken and thrown out of bed by the power of the Holy Spirit, you will dress yourself and be strong." I said this to him in faith. I laid hands on him in the name of Jesus and instantly the power of God fell and filled the place. I felt helpless and fell flat on the floor. I knew nothing except that a short while after the place was shaken; I heard the young man walking over me and saying, "For Thy glory, Lord! For Thy glory, Lord!"

He dressed himself and cried, "God has healed me." The father fell, the mother fell, and another who was present fell also. God manifested His power that day in saving the whole household and healing the young man. It is the power of the risen Christ we need. That young man is today preaching the gospel.

For years we have been longing for God to come forth, and, praise Him, He is coming forth. The tide is rising everywhere. I was in Switzerland not long ago, preaching in many places where the Pentecostal message had not been heard; and today there are nine new Pentecostal assemblies in different places going on blessedly for God. All over the world it is the same; this great Pentecostal work is in motion. You can hardly get to a place now where God is not pouring out His Spirit on hungry hearts. God has promised to pour out His Spirit upon all flesh, and His promises never fail. Our Christ is risen. His salvation was not a thing done in a corner. Truly He was a man of glory who went to Calvary for us in order that He might free us from all that would mar and hinder, that He might transform us by His grace and bring us out from under the power of Satan into the glorious power of God. One touch of our risen Christ will raise the dead. Hallelujah!

Oh, this wonderful Jesus of ours! He comes and indwells us. He comes to abide. He it is who baptizes us with the Holy Spirit and makes everything different. We are to be a kind of firstfruits unto God and are to be like Christ who is *the* firstfruit, walking in His footsteps, living in His power. What a salvation this is, having this risen Christ in us. I feel that everything else must go to nothingness, helplessness, and ruin. Every thought of advantage for ourselves must be on the decrease in order that Christ may increase, that we may live in another state where all things are under the power of the Spirit.

Dare you take your inheritance from God? Dare you believe God? Dare you stand on the record of His Word? What is the record? If thou shalt believe thou shalt see the glory of God. You will be sifted as wheat. You will be tried as though some strange thing tried you. You will be put in places where you will have to put your whole trust in God. There is no such thing as anyone being tried beyond what God will allow. Temptation will come, but God will be with you right in the temptation to deliver you; and when you have been tried, He will bring you forth as gold. Every trial is to bring you to a greater position in God. The trial that tries your faith will take you on to the place where you will know that the faith of God will be forthcoming in the next test. No man is able to win any victory except through the power of the risen Christ within him. You will never be able to say, "I

did this or that." You will desire to give God the glory
for everything.

If you are sure of your ground, if you are counting
on the presence of the living Christ within, you can
laugh when you see things getting worse. God would
have you settled and grounded in Christ, and it is
only as you are filled with the Holy Spirit that you become steadfast and unmoveable in Him.

The Lord Jesus said, "I have a baptism to be baptized with; and how am I straitened till it be accom-
plished!" He was assuredly straitened in the way, at
Gethsemane, at the judgment hall, and, after that, at
the cross, where He, through the eternal Spirit, of-
fered Himself without spot to God. God will lead us
in like manner every step of the way. God led Him
right through to the empty tomb, to the ascension
glory, to a place on the throne; and the Son of God
will never be satisfied until He has us with Himself,
sharing His glory and sharing His throne.

8

Righteousness

It is written of our blessed Lord, "Thou hast loved righteousness, and hated iniquity; therefore God, even thy God, hath anointed thee with the oil of gladness above thy fellows" (Hebrews 1:9). It is the purpose of God that we, as we are indwelt by the Spirit of His Son, should likewise love righteousness and hate iniquity. I see that there is a place for us in Christ Jesus where we are no longer under condemnation but where the heavens are always open to us. I see that God has a realm of divine life opening up to us where there are boundless possibilities, where there is limitless power, where there are untold resources, where we have victory over all the power of the devil. I believe that—as we are filled with the desire to press on into this life of true holiness, desiring only the glory of God—there is nothing that can hinder our true advancement.

Peter commences his second epistle with these words: "Simon Peter, a servant and an apostle of Jesus Christ, to them that have obtained like precious faith with us through the righteousness of God and our Saviour Jesus Christ." It is through faith we realize we have a blessed and glorious union with our risen Lord. When He was on earth, Jesus told us, "I am in the Father, and the Father in me." "The Father that dwelleth in me, He doeth the works." And He prayed to His Father, not only for His disciples but for those who should believe on Him through their word, "That they all may be one; as thou, Father, art in me, and I in thee, that they also may be one in us: that the world may believe that thou hast sent me" (John 17:21). Oh, what an inheritance is ours when the very nature, the very righteousness, the very power of the Father and the Son are made real in us. That is God's purpose, and as we by faith lay hold on the purpose we shall be ever conscious of the fact that greater is He that is in us than he that is in the world. The purpose of all Scripture is to move us on to this wonderful and blessed elevation of faith where our constant experience is the manifestation of God's life and power through us.

Peter goes on writing to these who have obtained like precious faith, saying, "Grace and peace be multiplied unto you through the knowledge of God, and of Jesus our Lord." We can have the multiplication of this grace and peace only as we live in the realm of faith. Abraham attained to the place where he became a friend of God, on no other line than that of believing God. He believed God and God counted that to him for righteousness. Righteousness was imputed to him on no other ground than that he believed God. Can this be true of anybody else? Yes, every person in the whole wide world who is saved by faith is blessed with faithful Abraham. The promise which came to him because he believed God was that in Him all the families of the earth should be blessed. When we believe God there is no knowing where the blessing of our faith will end.

Some are frustrated because when they are prayed for the thing that they are expecting does not come the same night. They say they believe, but you can see they are really in turmoil of unbelief. Abraham believed God. You can hear him saying to Sarah, "Sarah, there is no life in you and there is nothing in me, but God has promised us a son and I believe God." That kind of faith is a joy to our Father in heaven.

One day I was having a meeting in Bury, in Lancashire, England. A young woman was present to be healed of a goiter. Before she came she said, "I am going to be healed of this goiter, Mother." After one meeting she came forward and was prayed for. The next meeting she got up and testified that she had been wonderfully healed and she added, "I shall be so happy to go and tell Mother that I have been wonderfully healed." She went to her home and testified how wonderfully she had been healed, and the next year when we were having the convention she came again. To the natural view it looked as though the goiter was just as big as ever; but that young woman was believing God and she was soon on her feet giving her testimony, and saying, "I was here last year and the Lord wonderfully healed me. I want to tell you that this has been the best year of my life." She seemed to be greatly blessed in that meeting, and she went home to testify more strongly than ever that the Lord had healed her. She believed God. The third year she was at the meeting again, and some people who looked at her said, "How big that goiter has become." But when the testimony time came she was up on her feet and testified: "Two years ago the Lord graciously healed me of goiter. Oh I had a most wonderful healing. It is grand to be healed by the power of God." That day someone remonstrated with her and said, "People will think there is something the matter with you. Why don't you look in the mirror? You will see your goiter is bigger than ever." That good woman went to the

Lord about it and said, "Lord, you so wonderfully healed me two years ago. Won't you show all the people that you healed me." She went to sleep peacefully that night still believing God. The next day there was not a trace or a mark of that goiter.

God's word is from everlasting to everlasting. His word cannot fail. God's word is true; and when we rest in the fact of its truth, what mighty results we can get. Faith never looks in the mirror. Faith has a mirror into which it can look. It is the mirror of the perfect law of liberty. "Whoso looketh into the perfect law of liberty, and continueth therein, he being not a forgetful hearer, but a doer of the work, this man shall be blessed in his deed." To the man who looks into this perfect law of God all darkness is removed and he sees his completeness in Christ. There is no darkness in faith. There is only darkness in nature. Darkness only exists when the natural is put in the place of the divine.

Not only is grace multiplied to us through knowledge of God and of Jesus Christ, but peace also. As we really know our God and Jesus Christ whom He has sent, we will have peace multiplied to us even in the multiplied fires of ten thousand Nebuchadnezzars. It will be multiplied to us even though we are put into the den of lions, and we will live with joy in the midst of the whole thing. What was the difference between Daniel and the king that night when Daniel was put into the den of lions? Daniel knew, but the king was experimenting. The king came around the next morning and cried, "O Daniel, servant of the living God, is thy God, whom thou servest continually, able to deliver thee from the lions?" Daniel answered, "My God hath sent his angel, and hath shut the lions' mouths." The thing was done. It was done when Daniel prayed with his windows open toward heaven. All our victories are won before we go into the fight. Prayer links us to our lovely God, our abounding God, our multiplying God. Oh, I love Him! He is so wonderful!

You will note, as you read the first two verses of the first chapter of the second epistle of Peter, that this grace and peace is multiplied through the knowledge of God; but first our faith comes through the righteousness of God. Note that righteousness comes first and knowledge afterwards. It cannot be otherwise. If you expect any revelation of God apart from holiness, you will have only a mixture. Holiness opens the door to all the treasures of God. He must first bring us to the place where we, like our Lord, love righteousness and hate iniquity before He opens up to us these good treasures. When we regard iniquity in our hearts, the Lord will not hear us; and it is only as we are made righteous and pure and holy through the precious blood of God's Son that we can enter into this life of holiness and righteousness in the Son. It is the righteousness of our Lord Himself made real in us as our faith is stayed in Him.

After I was baptized with the Holy Spirit the Lord gave me a blessed revelation. I saw Adam and Eve turned out of the garden for their disobedience and unable to partake of the tree of life, for the cherubim with flaming sword kept them away from the tree. When I was baptized I saw that I had begun to eat of this tree of life and I saw that the flaming sword was all round about. It was there to keep the devil away. Oh, what privileges are ours when we are born of God. How marvelously He keeps us so that the wicked one touches us not. I see a place in God where Satan dare not come. Hidden in God. And He invites us all to come and share this wonderful hidden place where our lives are hid with Christ in God, where we dwell in the secret place of the Most High and abide under the shadow of the Almighty. God has this place for you in this blessed realm of grace.

Peter goes on to say, "According as his divine power hath given unto us all things that pertain unto life and godliness, through the knowledge of him that hath called us to glory and virtue." God is calling us to this realm of glory and virtue where, as we feed on His exceeding great and precious promises, we are made partakers of the divine nature. Faith is the substance of things hoped for right here in this life. It is right here that God would have us partake of His divine nature. It is nothing less than the life of the Lord Himself imparted and flowing into our whole beings, so that our very body is quickened, so that every tissue and every drop of blood and our bones and joints and marrow receive this divine life. I believe that the Lord wants this divine life to flow right into our natural bodies, this law of the spirit of life in Christ Jesus that makes us free from the law of sin and death. God wants to establish our faith so that we shall lay hold on this divine life, this divine nature of the Son of God, so that our spirit and soul and body will be sanctified wholly and preserved unto the coming of the Lord Jesus Christ.

When that woman was healed of the issue of blood, Jesus perceived that power had gone out of Him. The woman's faith laid hold and this power was imparted and immediately the woman's being was surcharged with life and her weakness departed. The impartation of this power produces everything you need; but it comes only as our faith moves out for its impartation. Faith is the victory. If you can believe, it is yours.

I suffered for many years from hemorrhoids till my whole body was thoroughly weak; the blood used to gush from me. One day I got desperate and I took a bottle of oil and anointed myself. I said to the Lord, "Do what you want to, quickly." I was healed at that very moment. God wants us to have an activity of faith that dares to believe God. There is what seems like faith, an appearance of faith, but real faith believes God right to the end.

What was the difference between Zacharias and Mary? The angel came to Zacharias, and told him, "Thy wife Elisabeth shall bear thee a son." Zacharias was there in the holy place, but he began to question this message, saying, "I am an old man, and my wife is well stricken in years." Gabriel rebuked him for his unbelief and told him, "Thou shalt be dumb, and not able to speak, until the day that these things shall be performed, because thou believest not my words." But note the contrast when the angel came to Mary. She said, "Behold the handmaid of the Lord; be it unto me according to thy word." And Elisabeth greeted Mary with the words, "Blessed is she that believed: for there shall be a performance of those things which were told her from the Lord." God would have us to lay hold on His word in like manner. He would have us come with boldness of faith, declaring, "You have promised it, Lord. *Now do it.*" God rejoices when we manifest a faith that holds Him to His word. Can we get there?

The Lord has called us to this glory and virtue; and as we believe Him, we shall see this in manifestation. I remember one day I was holding an open-air meeting. My uncle came to that meeting and said, "Aunt Mary would like to see Smith before she dies." I went to see her and she was dying. I said, "Lord, can't you do something?" All I did was stretch out my hands and lay them on her. It seemed as though there was an immediate impartation of the glory and virtue of the Lord. Aunt Mary cried, "It is going all over my body." And that day she was made perfectly whole.

One day I was preaching and a man brought a boy who was done up in bandages. The boy was in braces, and it was impossible for him to walk, and it was difficult for them to get him to the platform. They passed him over about six seats. The power of the Lord was present to heal and it entered right into the child as I placed my hands on him. The child cried, "Daddy, it is going all over me." They removed the braces and found nothing imperfect in him.

The Lord would have us to be walking epistles of His word. Jesus is the Word and is the power in us, and it is His desire to work in and through us His own good pleasure. We must believe that He is in us. There are boundless possibilities for us if we dare to act in God and dare to believe that the wonderful virtue of our living Christ shall be made manifest through us as we lay our hands on the sick in His name.

The exceeding great and precious promises of the Word are given to us that we might be partakers of the divine nature. I feel the Holy Spirit is grieved with us because, when we know these things, we do not do greater exploits for God. Does not the Holy Spirit show us wide-open doors of opportunity? Shall we not let God take us on to greater things? Shall we not believe God to take us on to greater manifestations of His power? His call for us is to forget the things that are behind, and reach forth unto the things which are before and to press toward the mark for the prize of the high calling of God in Christ Jesus.

9

The Words of This Life

Scripture Reading, Acts 5:1-20

Notice this expression that the Lord gives of the Gospel message—"the words of this life" (Acts 5:20). It is the most wonderful life possible—the life of faith in the Son of God. This is the life where God is all the time. He is round about and He is within. It is the life of many revelations and of many manifestations of God's Holy Spirit, a life in which the Lord is continually seen, known, felt and heard. It would take me a month to tell what there is in this wonderful life. Everyone can go in and possess and be possessed by this life.

It is possible for you to be within the vicinity of this life and yet miss it. It is possible for you to be in a place where God is pouring out His Spirit and yet miss the blessing that God is so willing to bestow. It all comes through shortness of revelation and through a misunderstanding of the infinite grace of God, and of the "God of all grace," who is willing to give to all who will reach out the hand of faith. This life that He freely bestows is a gift. Some think they have to earn it and they miss the whole thing. Oh, for a simple faith to receive all that God so lavishly offers. You can never be ordinary from the day you receive this life from above. You become extraordinary, filled with the extraordinary power of our extraordinary God.

83

Ananias and Sapphira were in this thing and yet they missed it. They were in the wonderful revival that God gave to the Early Church and yet they missed it. There are many people like them today who make vows to God in times of a great crisis in their lives. But they fail to keep their vows and in the end they become spiritually bankrupt. Blessed is the man who will swear to his own hurt and change not, who keeps the vow he has made to God, who is willing to lay his all at God's feet. The man who does this never becomes a lean soul. God has promised to "make fat his bones." There is no dry place for such a man; he is always spiritually fat and flourishing, and he becomes stronger and stronger. It pays to trust God with all and to make no reservation. I wish I could make you see how great a God we have.

Ananias and Sapphira were really doubting God and were questioning whether this work that He had begun would continue. They wanted to get some glory for selling their property, but because of their lack of faith they kept back part of the price in reserve in case the work of God should fail.

Many are doubting whether this Pentecostal revival will continue. Do you think this Pentecostal work will stop? Never. For fifteen years I have been in constant revival, and I am sure that it will never stop. When George Stephenson made his first engine he took his sister Mary to see it. She looked at it and said to her brother, "George, it'll never go." He said to her, "Get in, Mary." She said again, "It'll never go." He said to her, "We'll see, you get in." Mary at last got in—the whistle blew, there was a puff and a rattle, and the engine started off. Then Mary cried out, "George, it'll never stop! It'll never stop!"

People are looking at this Pentecostal revival, and

they are very critical and are saying, "It'll never go"; but when they are induced to come into the work, they all say, "It'll never stop." This revival of God is sweeping on and on and there is no stopping the current of life, of love, of inspiration, and of power. God has brought unlimited resources for everyone.

I want you to see that in the Early Church, controlled by the power of the Holy Spirit, it was not possible for a lie to exist. The moment it came into the church, there was instant death. And as the power of the Holy Spirit increases in these days of the revival, it will be impossible for any man to remain in our midst with a lying spirit. God will purify the church; the Word of God will be in such power in healing and other spiritual manifestations that great fear will be upon all those who see the same.

It seems to the natural mind a small thing for Ananias and Sapphira to want to have a little to fall back on; but I want to tell you that you can please God, and *you can get things from God only on the line of a living faith.* God never fails. God never can fail.

When I was in Bergen, Norway, there came to the meeting a young woman who was employed at the hospital as a nurse. A big cancer had developed on her nose, and the nose was enlarged and had become black and greatly inflamed. She came out for prayer and I said to her, "What is your condition?" She said, "I dare not touch my nose, it gives me so much pain." I said to all the people, "I want you to look at this nurse and notice her terrible condition. I believe that our God is merciful and that He is faithful and that He will bring to naught this condition that the devil has brought about. I am going to curse this disease in the all-powerful name of Jesus. The pain will go. I believe God will give us an exhibition of His grace and I will ask this young woman to come to the meeting to-morrow night and declare what God has done for her."

Oh, the awfulness of sin! Oh, the awfulness of the power of sin! Oh, the awfulness of the consequences of the fall! When I see a cancer I always know it is an evil spirit. I can never believe it is otherwise. The same with tumors. Can this be the work of God? God help me to show you that this is the work of the devil and to show you the way out.

I do not condemn people that sin. I don't scold people. I know what is back of the sin. I know that Satan is always going about as a roaring lion, seeking whom he may devour. I always remember the patience and love of the Lord Jesus Christ. When they brought to Him a woman that they had taken in adultery, telling Him that they had caught her in the very act, He simply stooped down and wrote on the ground. Then He quietly said, "He that is without sin among you, let him first cast a stone." I have never seen a man without sin. "All have sinned and come short of the glory of God." But I read in this blessed gospel message that God hath laid upon Jesus the iniquity of us all; so, when I see an evil condition, I feel that I must stand in my office and rebuke the condition.

I laid my hands on the nose of the suffering nurse and cursed the evil power that was causing her so much distress. The next night the place was packed and the people were jammed together, so that it seemed that there was not room for one more to get in. How God's rain fell upon us. How good God is, so full of grace and so full of love. I saw the nurse in the audience and I asked her to come forward. She came and showed everyone what God had done. He had perfectly healed her. Oh, I tell you He is just the same Jesus. He is just the same today. All things are possible if you dare to trust God.

When the power of God came so mightily upon the Early Church, even in the death of Ananias and Sapphira, great fear came upon all the people. And when we are in the presence of God, when God is working mightily in our midst, there comes a great fear, a reverence, a holiness of life, a purity that fears to displease God. We read that no man durst join them, but God added to the church such as should be saved. I would rather have God add to our Pentecostal church than have all the town join it. God added daily to His own church.

The next thing that happened was that people became so assured that God was working that they knew that anything would be possible, and they brought their sick into the streets and laid them on beds and couches, that at least the shadow of Peter passing by might overshadow them. Multitudes of sick people and those oppressed with evil spirits were brought to the apostles and God healed them every one. I do not believe that it was the shadow of Peter that healed, but the power of God was mightily present and the faith of the people was so aroused that they joined with one heart to believe God. God will always meet people on the line of faith.

God's tide is rising all over the earth. I had been preaching at Stavanger in Norway, and was very tired and wanted a few hours rest. I went to my next appointment, arriving at about 9:30 in the morning. My first meeting was to be at night. I said to my interpreter, "After we have had something to eat, let us go down to the fjords." We spent three or four hours down by the sea and at about 4:30 returned. We found the end of the street, which has a narrow en-

trance, filled with autos, wagons, and containing in-
valids and sick people of every kind. I went up to the
house and was told that the house was full of sick
people. It reminded me of the scene described in the
fifth chapter of Acts. I began praying for the people in
the street and God began to heal the people. How
wonderfully He healed those people who were in the
house. We sat down for a lunch and the telephone
bell rang and someone at the other end was saying,
"What shall we do? The town hall is already full; the
police cannot control things."

In that little Norwegian town the people were
jammed together, and oh, how the power of God fell
upon us. A cry went up from every one, "Isn't this the
revival?"

Revival is coming. The breath of the Almighty is
coming. The breath of God shows up every defect,
and as it comes flowing in like a river, everybody will
need a fresh anointing, a fresh cleansing of the blood.
That breath is upon us.

At one time I was at a meeting in Ireland. There
were many sick carried to that meeting and helpless
ones were helped there. There were many people in
that place who were seeking for the baptism of the
Holy Ghost. Some of them had been seeking for years.
There were sinners there who were under mighty
conviction. There came a moment when *the breath of
God swept through the meeting*. In about ten minutes
every sinner in the place was saved. Everyone who
had been seeking the Holy Spirit was baptized, and
every sick one was healed. God is a reality and His
power can never fail. As our faith reaches out, God
will meet us and the same rain will fall. It is the same
blood that cleanseth, the same power, the same Holy
Spirit, and the same Jesus made real through the

power of the Holy Spirit! What would happen if we should believe God?

Right now the precious blood of the Lord Jesus Christ is efficacious to cleanse your heart and bring this life, this wonderful life of God within you. The blood will make you every whit whole if you dare believe. The Bible is full of entreaty for you to come and partake and receive the grace, the power, the strength, the righteousness, and the full redemption of Jesus Christ. He never fails to hear when we believe.

At one place where I was, a lame man was brought to me who had been in bed for two years, with no hope of recovery. He was brought thirty miles to the meeting, and he came up on crutches to be prayed for. His boy was also afflicted in the knees and they had four crutches between the two of them. The man's face was filled with torture. There is healing virtue in the Lord and He never fails to heal when we believe. In the name of Jesus—that name so full of virtue—I put my hand down that leg that was so diseased. The man threw down his crutches and all were astonished as they saw him walking up and down without aid. The little boy called out to his father, "Papa, me; papa, me, me, me!" The little boy who was withered in both knees wanted a like touch. And the same Jesus was there to bring a real deliverance for the little captive. He was completely healed.

These were legs that were touched. If God will stretch out His mighty power to loose afflicted legs, what mercy will He extend to that soul of yours that must exist forever? Hear the Lord say, "The Spirit of the Lord is upon me, because he hath anointed me to preach the gospel to the poor; he hath sent me to heal the broken hearted, to preach deliverance to the captive, and recovering of sight to the blind, to set at liberty them that are bruised." He invites you, "Come unto me, all ye that labor and are heavy laden, and I will give you rest." God is willing in His great mercy to touch your limbs with His mighty power; and if He is willing to do this, how much more anxious is He to deliver thee from the power of Satan and to make thee a child of the King. How much more necessary it is for you to be healed of your soul sickness than of your bodily ailments. And God is willing to give the double cure.

I was passing through the city of London one time, and Mr. Mundell, the secretary of the Pentecostal Missionary Union, learned that I was there. He arranged for me to meet him at a certain place at 3:30 p.m. I was to meet a certain boy whose father and mother lived in the city of Salisbury. They had sent this young man to London to take care of their business. He had been a leader in Sunday school work, but he had been betrayed and had fallen. Sin is awful and the wages of sin is death. But there is another side—the gift of God is eternal life.

This young man was in great distress; he had contracted a horrible disease and feared to tell anyone. There was nothing but death ahead for him. When the father and mother got to know of his condition they suffered inexpressible grief.

When we got to the house, Brother Mundell suggested, that we get down to prayer. I said, "God does not say so, we are not going to pray yet. I want to quote a scripture: 'Fools because of their transgression, and because of their iniquities, are afflicted. Their soul abhorreth all manner of meat; and they draw near unto the gates of death'" (Psalm 107:17,18). The young man cried out, "I am that fool." He broke down and told us the story of his fall. Oh, if men would only repent, and confess their sins, how God would stretch out His hand to heal and to save. The moment that young man repented, a great abscess burst, and God sent virtue into his life, giving him a mighty deliverance.

God is gracious and not willing that any should perish. How many are willing to make a clean breast of their sins? I tell you that the moment you do this, God will open heaven. It is an easy thing for Him to save your soul and heal your disease if you will but come and shelter today in the secret place of the Most High. He will satisfy you with long life and show you His salvation. In His presence there is fullness of joy, at His right hand there are pleasures forevermore. There is full redemption for all through the precious blood of the Son of God.

10

Life in the Spirit

Scripture Reading, 2 Corinthians 3

We are told that we are to leave the first principles of the doctrine of Christ and go on to perfection, not laying again the foundation of repentance from dead works and the doctrine of baptisms and other first principles (Hebrews 6). What would you think of a builder who was everlastingly pulling down his house and putting in fresh foundations? *Never look back if you want the power of God in your life.* You will find out that in the measure you have allowed yourself to look back you have missed that which God has for you.

The Holy Spirit shows us that we must never look back to the law of sin and death from which we have been delivered. God has brought us into a new order of things, a life of love and liberty in Christ Jesus that is beyond all human comprehension. Many are brought into this new life through the power of the Spirit of God, and then, like the Galatians, who ran well at the beginning, they try to perfect themselves on the lines of legalism. They go back from the life in the Spirit to a life on natural lines. God is not pleased with this, for He has no place for the man who has lost the vision. The only thing to do is to repent. Don't try to cover up anything. If you have been tripped up on any line, confess it out, and then look to

God to bring you to a place of stability of faith where your whole walk will be in the Spirit.

We all ought to have a clear conviction *that salvation is of the Lord*. It is more than a human order of things. If the enemy can move you from a place of faith, he can get you outside the plan of God. The moment a man falls into sin, divine life ceases to flow, and his life becomes one of helplessness. But this is not God's thought for any of His children. Read the third chapter of John's first epistle and take your place as a son of God. Take the place of knowing that you are a son of God; and remember that as your hope is set in Christ, it should have a purifying effect on your life. The Holy Spirit says, "Whosoever is born of God doth not commit sin; for His seed remaineth in him: and he cannot sin, because he is born of God." There is life and power in the seed of the Word that is implanted within. God is in that *"cannot,"* and there is more power in that word of His than in any human objections. God's thought for everyone of us is that we shall reign in life by Jesus Christ. You must come to see how wonderful you are in God and how helpless you are in yourself.

God declared Himself more mighty than every opposing power when He cast out the powers of darkness from heaven. I want you to know that the same power that cast Satan out of heaven dwells in every man that is born of God. If you would but realize this, you would reign in life. When you see people bound by an evil power, when you see the powers of evil manifesting themselves, always put the question, "Did Jesus come in the flesh?" I have never seen an evil power answer in the affirmative. When you know you have an evil spirit to deal with you have power to cast it out. Believe it and act on it, for "greater is he that is in you, than he that is in the world" (1 John 4:4). God means for you to be in a place of overcoming, and has put a force within you whereby you may defeat the devil.

Temptations will come to all. If you are not worth tempting you are not worth powder and shot. Job said: "When He hath tried me, I shall come forth as gold." In every temptation that comes, the Lord lets you be tempted up to the very hilt, but will never allow you to be defeated if you walk in obedience; for right in the midst of the temptation He will always "make a way of escape."

May God help us to see it. We cannot be to the praise of His glory until we are ready for trials, and are able to triumph in them. We cannot get away from the fact that sin came in by nature, but God comes into our nature and puts it into the place of death that the Spirit of God may come into the temple in all His power and liberty, that right here in this present evil world Satan may be dethroned by the believer.

Satan is always endeavoring to bring the saints of God into disrepute, bringing against them railing accusations, but the Holy Spirit never comes with condemnation. He always reveals the blood of Christ. He always brings us help. The Lord Jesus referred to Him as the Comforter who would come. He is always on hand to help in the seasons of trial and test. The Holy Spirit is the lifting power of the church of Christ. And Paul tells us that we "are manifestly declared to be the epistle of Christ . . . written not with ink, but with the Spirit of the living God; not in tables of stone, but in fleshly tables of the heart." The Holy Spirit begins in the heart, right in the depths of human affections. He brings into the heart the riches of the revelation of Christ, implanting purity and holiness there, so that, out of its depths, praises may well up continually.

The Holy Spirit will make us epistles of Christ, ever telling out that Jesus our Lord is our Redeemer; and God has never put away that revelation. And because of the perfect atonement of that slain Lamb, there is salvation, healing, and deliverance for all. Some people think that they have only to be cleansed once; but as we walk in the light, the blood of Jesus Christ is ever cleansing.

The very life of Christ has been put within us and is moving within us—a perfect life. May the Lord help us to see the power of this life. The years of a man's life are threescore and ten, and so in the natural order of things, my life will be finished in seven years, but I have begun a new life that will never end. "From everlasting to everlasting Thou art God." This is the life I have come into, and there is no end to this life. In me is working a power stronger than every other power; Christ, the power of God, formed within me. I can see why we need to be clothed upon from above, for the life that is in me is a thousand times bigger than I am outside. There must be a tremendous expansion. I see that this thing cannot be understood on natural lines; no natural reason can comprehend the divine plan.

We are not sufficient to think anything as of ourselves, but our sufficiency is of God (2 Corinthians 3:5). If you go back, you miss the plan. We leave the old order of things. We can never have confidence in the flesh; we cannot touch that. We are in a new order, a spiritual order. It is a new life of absolute faith in the sufficiency of our God in everything that pertains to life and godliness.

Paul further tells us that He has made us "able ministers of the new testament; not of the letter, but of the spirit: for the letter killeth, but the spirit giveth life" (2 Corinthians 3:6). It is one thing to read this, and another to have the revelation of it and to see the spiritual force of it. Any man can live in the letter and become dry and wordy, limited in knowledge of spiritual verities, and spend his time everlastingly in splitting hairs; but as soon as he touches the realm of the Spirit, all the dryness goes, all the spirit of criticism leaves. There can be no divisions in a life in the Spirit. The Spirit of God brings such pliability and such love! There is no love like the love in the Spirit. It is a pure, a holy, a divine love that is shed in our hearts by the Spirit. It loves to serve and to honor the Lord.

I can never estimate what the baptism of the Holy Ghost has been to me these past fifteen years. It seems that every year has had three years packed into it, so that I have had forty-five years of happy service since 1907. And it is getting better all the time. It is a luxury to be filled with the Spirit, and at the same time it is a divine command for us, not to be filled with wine wherein is excess, but to be filled with the Spirit. No Pentecostal person ought to get out of bed without being lost in the Spirit and speaking in tongues as the Spirit gives utterance. No one should come into the door of an assembly without speaking in tongues or having a psalm or a note of praise. We emphasize that at the incoming of the Spirit He should so fill us that the last member in the body is yielded to Him and that no one is baptized in the Spirit without speaking in tongues as the Spirit gives utterance; and I maintain that with a *constant filling* you will speak in tongues morning, noon and night. As you live in the Spirit, when you walk down the

steps of the house where you live, the devil will have
to go before you. You will be more than a conqueror
over the devil.

I see everything a failure except that which is done
in the Spirit. But as you live in the Spirit, you move,
act, eat, drink, and do everything to the glory of God.
Our message is always this, "Be filled with the Spirit."
This is God's place for you, and it is as far above the
natural life as the heavens are above the earth. Yield
yourselves for God to fill.

Moses had a tremendous trial with the people.
They were always in trouble. But as he went up into
the mount, and God unfolded to him the ten commandments, the glory fell. He rejoiced to bring those
two tables of stone down from the mount, and his
very countenance shone with the glory. He was bringing to Israel that which, if obeyed, would bring life.

I think of my Lord coming from heaven. I think all
heaven was moved by the sight. The law of the letter
was brought by Moses and it was made glorious, but
all its glory of Sinai paled before the glory of Pentecost. Those tables of stone with their "Thou shalt not,
thou shalt not," are done away; for they never
brought life to anyone, and the Lord has brought in a
new covenant, putting His law in our minds and writing it in our hearts, this new law of the Spirit of life.
As the Holy Ghost comes in, He fills us with such love
and liberty that we shout for joy these words of this
11th verse, "Done away! Done away!" Henceforth
there is a new cry in our hearts, *"I delight to do Thy
will, O God."* He taketh away the first, the ministration of death, written and engraven in stones, that He
might establish the second, this ministration of righteousness, this life in the Spirit.

You ask, "Does a man who is filled with the Spirit

cease to keep the commandments?" I simply repeat
what the Spirit of God has told us here, that this ministration of death, written and engraven in stones is
DONE AWAY. The man who becomes a living epistle
of Christ, written with the Spirit of the living God,
has ceased to be an adulterer, or a murderer or a covetous man; the will of God is his delight. I love to do
the will of God; there is no irksomeness to it; it is no
trial to pray; no trouble to read the Word of God; it is
not a hard thing to go to the place of worship. With
the psalmist you say, "I was glad when they said unto
me, Let us go into the house of the Lord."

How does this new life work out? The thing works
out because God works in you to will and to do of His
own good pleasure (Philippians 2:13). There is a
great difference between a pump and a spring. The
law is a pump, the Baptism is a spring. The old pump
gets out of order, the parts perish, and the well runs
dry. The letter killeth. But the spring is ever bubbling
up and there is a ceaseless flow direct from the throne
of God. There is life.

It is written of Christ, "Thou lovest righteousness,
and hatest wickedness." And in this new life in the
Spirit, in this new covenant life, you love the things
that are right and pure and holy, and shudder at all
things that are wrong. Jesus was able to say, "The
prince of this world cometh, and hath nothing in me,"
and the moment we are filled with the Spirit of God
we are brought into like wonderful condition, and, as
we continue to be filled with the Spirit, the enemy
cannot have an inch of territory in us.

Do you not believe that you can be so filled with
the Spirit that a man who is not living right can be
judged and convicted by your presence? As we go on
in the life of the Spirit it will be said of us, "in whose

eyes a vile person is contemned" (Psalm 15:4). Jesus lived there and moved in this realm, and His life was a constant reproof to the wickedness around Him. But He was the Son of God, you say. God, through Him, has brought us into the place of sonship, and I believe that if He has a chance with the material, the Holy Ghost can make something of us and bring us to the same place.

I don't want to boast. If I glory in anything, it is only in the Lord who has been so gracious to me. But I remember one time stepping out of a railroad car to wash my hands. I had a season of prayer, and the Lord just filled me to overflowing with His love. I was going to a convention in Ireland, and I could not get there fast enough. As I returned, I believe that the Spirit of the Lord was so heavily upon me that my face must have shone. (No man can tell himself when the Spirit transforms his very countenance.) There were two clerical men sitting together, and as I got into the carriage again, one of them cried out, "You convince me of sin." Within three minutes everyone in the car was crying to God for salvation. This thing has happened many times in my life. It is this ministration of the Spirit that Paul speaks of, this filling of the Spirit that will make your life effective so that even the people in the stores where you trade will want to leave your presence because they are brought under conviction.

We must move from everything of the letter. All that we do must be done *under the anointing of the Spirit*. The trouble has been that we as Pentecostal people have been living in the letter. Believe what the Holy Spirit says through Paul—that all this ministration of condemnation that has hindered your liberty in Christ is *done away*. The law is DONE AWAY! As far as you are concerned, all that old order of things is forever done away, and the Spirit of God has brought in a new life of purity and love. The Holy Spirit takes it for granted that you are finished with all the things of the old life when you become a new creation in Christ. In the life in the Spirit, the old allurements have lost their power. The devil will meet you at every turn, but the Spirit of God will always lift up a standard against him.

Oh, if God had His way, we should be like torches, purifying the very atmosphere wherever we go, moving back the forces of wickedness.

Done away! What do I mean? Will you be disloyal? You will be more than loyal. Will you grumble when you are treated badly? No, you will turn the other cheek. This is what you will always do when God lives in you. Leave yourselves in God's hands. Enter into rest. "He that is entered into his rest, he also hath ceased from his own works, as God did from his" (Hebrews 4:10). O this is a lovely rest! The whole life is a Sabbath. This is the only life that can glorify God. It is a life of joy, and every day is a day of heaven on earth.

There is a continual transformation in this life. Beholding the Lord and His glory we are changed into the same image from glory to glory, even by the Spirit of the Lord. There is a continual unveiling, a constant revelation, a repeated clothing upon from above. I want you to promise God never to look back, never to go back to that which the Spirit has said is "done away." I made this promise to the Lord that I would never allow myself to doubt His Word.

A baby takes all that comes to it. A prudent man lets his reason cheat him out of God's best. But a baby takes all that its mother brings and tries to swallow the bottle and all. The baby can't walk, but the mother carries it; the baby cannot dress itself, but the mother dresses it. The baby can't even talk. So in the life of the Spirit, God undertakes to do what we cannot do. We are carried along by Him, He clothes us, and He gives us utterance. Would that we all had the simplicity of the babes.

11

What It Means to Be Full of the Spirit

Scripture Reading, Acts 6

In the days when the number of disciples began to be multiplied there developed a situation which caused the Twelve to make a definite decision not to occupy themselves with serving tables, but to give themselves continually to prayer and to the ministry of the Word. How important it is for all of God's ministers to be continually in prayer and feeding on the Scriptures of Truth. I always take my Bible or New Testament with me.

None of you can be strong in God unless you diligently hearken to what God has to say to you through His Word. You cannot know the power and the nature of God unless you partake of His inbreathed Word. Read it at morn and at night and at every opportunity you get. After every meal, instead of indulging in unprofitable conversation round the table, read a chapter from the Word and then have a season of prayer. I endeavor to make a point of doing this no matter where or with whom I am staying.

The Psalmist said that he had hid God's Word in his heart, that he might not sin against Him; and you will find that the more of God's Word you hide in your heart, the easier it is to live a holy life. He also testified that God's Word had quickened him; and as you receive God's Word into your being, your whole physical being will be quickened and you will be made strong. As you receive with meekness the Word, you will find faith springing up within. And you will have life through the Word.

The Twelve told the rest to find seven men to look after the business end of things. They were to be men of honest report and filled with the Holy Spirit. These were just ordinary men who were chosen, but they were filled with the Holy Spirit; and this infilling always lifts a man to a plane above the ordinary. It does not take a cultured or a learned man to fill a position in God's church; what God requires is a yielded, consecrated, holy life, and He can make of such a flame of fire. Baptized with the Holy Spirit and fire!

The multitude chose out seven men to serve tables. They were doubtless faithful in their appointed tasks, but we see that God soon had a better choice for two of them. Philip was so full of the Holy Spirit that he could have a revival wherever God put him down. Man chose him to serve tables, but God chose him to win souls. Oh, if I could only stir you up to see that as you are faithful in performing the humblest office, God can fill you with His Spirit and make you a chosen vessel for Himself and promote you to a place of mighty ministry in the salvation of souls and in the healing of the sick. There is nothing impossible to a man filled with the Holy Spirit. It is beyond all human comprehension. When you are filled with the power of the Holy Spirit, God will wonderfully work wherever you go.

When you are filled with the Spirit you will know the voice of God. I want to give you one illustration of this. When I was going to Australia recently, our boat stopped at Aden and at Bombay. In the first place the people came round the ship selling their

wares, beautiful carpets and all sorts of oriental
things. There was one man selling some ostrich feathers. As I was looking over the side of the ship watch-
ing the trading, a gentleman said to me, "Would you
go shares with me in buying that bunch of feathers?"
What did I want with feathers? I had no use for such
things and no room for them either. But the gentleman put the question to me again, "Will you go
shares with me in buying that bunch?" The Spirit of
God said to me, "Do it."

The price of the feathers was three pounds, but
the gentleman said, "I have no money with me, but if
you will pay the man for them, I will send the cash
down to you by the purser." I paid for the feathers
and gave the gentleman his share. I said to him, "No,
please don't give that money to the purser, I want you
to bring it to me personally to my cabin." I said to the
Lord, "What about these feathers?" He showed me
that He had a purpose in my purchasing them.

At about ten o'clock the gentleman came to my
cabin and said, "I've brought the money." I said to
him, "It is not your money that I want, it is your soul
that I am seeking for God." Right there he opened up
the whole plan of his life and began to seek God; and
that morning he wept his way through to God's salvation.

You have no idea what God can do through you
when you are filled with His Spirit. Every day and
every hour you can have the divine leading of God.
To be filled with the Holy Spirit means much in every
way. I have seen some who have been suffering for
years, and when they have been filled with the Holy
Spirit all of their sickness has passed away. The Spirit
of God has made real to them the life of Jesus, and

they have been completely liberated of every sickness and infirmity.

Look at Stephen. He was just an ordinary man chosen to serve tables. But the Holy Spirit was in him and he was full of faith and power and did great wonders and miracles among the people. There was no resisting the wisdom and the spirit by which he spake. How important it is that every man be filled with the Holy Spirit.

I want to impress the importance of this upon you. It is not healing that I am presenting to you—it is the living Christ. It is a glorious fact that the Son of God came down to bring liberty to the captives.

How is it that the moment you are filled with the Holy Spirit persecution starts? It was so with the Lord Jesus Himself. We do not read of any persecutions before the Holy Spirit came down like a dove upon Him. Shortly after this, after preaching in His home town, they wanted to throw Him over the brow of a hill. It was the same with the twelve disciples. They had no persecution before the day of Pentecost; but after they were filled with the Spirit, they were soon in prison. The devil and the priests of religion will always get stirred when a man is filled with the Spirit and does things in the power of the Spirit. And persecution is the greatest blessing to a church. When we have persecution we will have purity. If you desire to be filled with the Spirit, you can count on persecution. The Lord came to bring division, and even in your own household you may find three against two.

The Lord Jesus came to bring peace; and soon after you get peace within, you get persecution without. If you remain stationary, the devil and his agents will not disturb you much. But when you press on with

God, the enemy has you as a target. But God will vindicate you in the midst of the whole thing.

At a meeting I was holding, the Lord was working and many were being healed. A man saw what was taking place and remarked, "I'd like to try this thing." He came up for prayer and told me that his body was broken in two places. I laid my hands on him in the name of the Lord, and said to him, "Now, you believe God." The next night he was at meeting and he got up like a lion. He said, "I want to tell you people that this man here is deceiving you. He laid his hands on me last night for rupture in two places, but I'm not a bit better." I stopped him and said, "You are healed, your trouble is that you won't believe it."

He was at meeting the next night and when there was opportunity for testimony this man arose. He said, "I'm a mason by trade. Today I was working with a laborer and he had to put a big stone in place. I helped him and did not feel any pain. I said to myself, 'How have I done it?' I found I was healed." I told the people, "Last night this man was against the Word of God, but now he believes it. It is true that these signs shall follow them that believe, they shall lay hands on the sick and they shall recover. And all through the power that is in the name of Christ." It is the Spirit who has come to reveal the Word of God and to make it spirit and life to us.

You who are seeking the Baptism are entering a place where you will have persecution. Your best friends will leave you—or those you may esteem your best friends. No *good* friend will ever leave you. But it is worthwhile. You enter into a realm of illumination, or revelation, by the power of the Holy Spirit. He reveals the preciousness and the power of the blood of Christ. I find by the revelation of the Spirit that there is not one thing in me that the blood does not cleanse. I find that God sanctifies me by the blood and reveals that efficacy of the work by the Spirit.

Stephen was just an ordinary man clothed with the divine. He was full of faith and power, and great wonders and miracles were wrought by him. Oh, this life in the Holy Spirit! this life of deep, inward revelation, of transformation from one state to another, of growing in grace and in all knowledge and in the power of the Spirit, the life and the mind of Christ being renewed in you, and of constant revelations of the might of His power. It is the only kind of thing that will enable us to stand.

In this life the Lord puts you in all sorts of places and then reveals His power. I had been preaching in New York, and sailed one day for England on the Lusitania. As soon as I got on board I went down to my cabin. Two men were there, and one of them said, "Well, will I do for company?" He took out a bottle and poured out a glass of whiskey and drank it, and then he filled it up for me. "I never touch that stuff," I said. "How can you live without it?" he asked. "How could I live with it?" I asked. He admitted, "I have been under the influence of this stuff for months, and they say my inside is all shrivelled up, and I know that I am dying. I wish I could be delivered, but I just have to keep on drinking. Oh, if I could only be delivered! My father died in England and has given me his fortune, but what will the good of it be to me except to hasten me to my grave?"

I said to this man, "Say the word, and you will be delivered." He asked, "What do you mean?" I said, "Say the word, show that you are willing to be delivered and God will deliver you." But it was just as if I were talking to this platform for all the comprehen-

sion he showed. I said to him, "Stand still," and I laid
my hands on his head in the name of Jesus and cursed
that drink demon that was taking his life. He cried
out, "I'm free! I'm free! I know I'm free!" He took two
bottles of whiskey and threw them overboard, and
God saved, sobered, and healed him. I was preaching
all the way across. He sat beside me at the table. Previous to this he had not been able to eat; but at every
meal he went right through the menu. You only have
to have a touch from Jesus to have a good time. The
power of God is just the same today. To me, He's
lovely. To me, He's saving health. To me, He's the lily
of the valley. Oh, this blessed Nazarene, this King of
kings! Hallelujah! Will you let Him have your will?
Will you let Him have *you*? If you will, all His power
is at your disposal.

They were not able to resist the wisdom and spirit
by which Stephen spake, and so, full of rage, they
brought him to the council. And God filled his face
with a ray of heaven's light. It is worth being filled
with the Spirit, no matter what it costs. Read the sev-
enth chapter of Acts, the mighty prophetic utterance
by this holy man. Without fear he tells them, "Ye
stiffnecked and uncircumcised in heart and ears, ye
do always resist the Holy Ghost." And when they
heard these things they were cut to the heart. There
are two ways of being affected at the heart. Here they
gnashed their teeth and cast him out of the city and
stoned him. On the day of Pentecost, when they were
pricked at the heart they cried out, "What shall we
do?" They took the opposite way. The devil, if he can
have his way, will cause you to commit murder. If
Jesus has His way, you will repent.

And Stephen, full of the Holy Spirit, looked up
steadfastly into heaven, and saw the glory of God,

and the Son of man standing on the right hand of God. Oh, this being full of the Holy Spirit! How much it means. I was riding for sixty miles one summer day and as I looked up in the heavens I had an open vision of Jesus all the way. It takes the Holy Spirit to give this.

Stephen cried out, "Lord, lay not this sin to their charge." As he was full of the Spirit he was full of love, and he manifested the very same compassion for his enemies that Jesus did at Calvary. Being filled with the Holy Spirit means much in every way. It means constant filling, quickening, and a new life continually. Oh, it's lovely! We have a wonderful gospel and a great Saviour! If you will but be filled with the Holy Spirit, you will have a constant spring within; yes, as your faith centers in the Lord Jesus, from within you shall flow rivers of living water.

12

The Bible Evidence of the Baptism in the Spirit

There is much controversy today regarding the genuineness of the Pentecostal work, but there is nothing so convincing as the fact that over fifteen years ago (1907) a Holy Spirit revival began and has never ceased. You will find that in every clime throughout the world God has poured out His Spirit in a remarkable way in a line parallel with the glorious revival that inaugurated the church of the first century. People, who could not understand what God was doing when He kept them concentrated in prayer, wondered as these days were being brought about by the Holy Spirit. They found themselves in exactly the same place and entered into an identical experience as the Apostles on the day of Pentecost.

Our Lord Jesus said to His disciples, "Behold, I send the promise of my Father upon you: but tarry ye in the city of Jerusalem, until ye be endued with power from on high" (Luke 24:49). God promised through the prophet Joel, "I will pour out my spirit upon *all flesh.* . . . upon the servants and upon the handmaids in those days will I pour out my spirit." As there is a widespread misconception concerning this receiving of the Holy Spirit, I believe the Lord would have us examine the Scriptures on this subject.

It had to be something on the line of solid facts to move me. I was as certain as possible that I had received the Holy Spirit and was absolutely rigid in this conviction. When this Pentecostal outpouring began in England I went to Sunderland and met with the people who had assembled for the purpose of receiving the Holy Spirit. I was continually in those meetings causing disturbances until the people wished I had never come. They said that I was disturbing the conditions for receiving the Holy Spirit. But I was hungry and thirsty for God and had gone to Sunderland because I heard that God was pouring out His Spirit in a new way. I heard that God had now visited His people, had manifested His power and that people were speaking in tongues as on the day of Pentecost.

When I got to this place I said, "I cannot understand this meeting. I have left a meeting in Bradford all on fire for God. The fire fell last night and we were all laid out under the power of God. I have come here for tongues, and I don't hear them—I don't hear anything."

"Oh!" they said, "when you get baptized with the Holy Spirit you will speak in tongues." "Oh, is that it?" said I, "when the presence of God came upon me, my tongue was loosened, and really I felt as I went in the open air to preach that I had a new tongue." "Ah, no," they said, "When you get baptized in the Holy Spirit—" "I am baptized," I interjected, "and there is no one here who can persuade me that I am not baptized." So I was up against them and they were up against me.

I remember a man getting up and saying, "You know, brothers and sisters, I was here three weeks and then the Lord baptized me with the Holy Spirit and I began to speak with other tongues." I said, "Let us hear it. That's what I'm here for." But he would not talk in tongues. I was doing what others are doing today, confusing 1 Corinthians 12 with the Acts 2. These two chapters deal with different things, one with the gifts of the Spirit and the other with the baptism of the Spirit with the accompanying sign. I did not understand this and so I said to the man, "Let's hear you speak in tongues." But he could not. He had not received the "gift" of tongues, but the Baptism.

As the days passed I became more and more hungry. I had opposed the meetings so much, but the Lord was gracious, and I shall ever remember that last day—the day I was to leave. God was with me so much that last night. They were to have a meeting and I went, but I could not rest. I went to the Vicarage, and there in the library I said to Mrs. Boddy, "I cannot rest any longer, I must have these tongues." She replied, "Brother Wigglesworth, it is not the tongues you need but the Baptism. If you will allow God to baptize you, the other will be all right." "My dear sister, I know I *am* baptized," I said. "You know that I have to leave here at four o'clock. Please lay hands on me that I may receive the tongues."

She rose up and laid her hands on me and *the fire fell. I said, "The fire's falling."* Then came a persistent knock at the door, and she had to go out. That was the best thing that could have happened, for I was ALONE WITH GOD. Then He gave me a revelation. Oh, it was wonderful! He showed me an empty cross and Jesus glorified. I do thank God that the cross is empty, that Christ is no more on the cross. It was there that He bore the curse, for it is written, "Cursed is everyone that hangeth on a tree." He became sin for us that we might be made the righteousness of God in Him, and now, there He is in the glory. Then I saw that God had purified me. It seemed that God gave me a new vision, and I saw a perfect being wihin me with mouth open, saying, "Clean! Clean! Clean!" When I began to repeat it I found myself speaking in other tongues. The joy was so great that when I came to utter it my tongue failed, and I began to worship God in other tongues as the Spirit gave me utterance.

It was all as beautiful and peaceful as when Jesus said, "Peace, be still!" and the tranquillity of that moment and the joy surpassed anything I had ever known up to that moment. But, hallelujah! these days have grown with greater, mightier, more wonderful divine manifestations and power. That was but the beginning. There is no end to this kind of beginning. The experiences in the Holy Spirit will not end until you are in heaven—till you are right in the presence of God forever. And even then we shall ever be conscious of His presence.

What had I received? I had received the Bible evidence. This Bible evidence is wonderful to me. I knew I had received the very evidence of the Spirit's incoming that the Apostles received on the Day of Pentecost. I knew that everything I had had up to that time was in the nature of an anointing bringing me in line with God in preparation, but now I knew I had the biblical baptism in the Spirit. It had the backing of the Scriptures. You are always right when you have the backing of the Scriptures, and you are never right if you have not a foundation for your testimony in the Word of God.

For many years I have thrown out a challenge to any person who can prove to me that he has the Baptism without speaking in tongues as the Spirit gives utterance—to prove it by the Word that he has been baptized in the Holy Spirit without the Bible evidence—but so far no one has accepted the challenge. I only say this because so many are as I was; they

have a rigid idea that they have received the Baptism
without the Bible evidence. The Lord Jesus wants
those who preach the Word to have the Word in evidence. Don't be misled by anything else. Have a Bible
proof for all you have, and then you will be in a place
where no man can move you.

I was so full of joy that I wired home to say that I
had received the Holy Spirit. As soon as I got home,
my boy came running up to me and said, "Father,
have you received the Holy Spirit?" I said, "Yes, my
boy." He said, "Let's hear you speak in tongues." But
I could not. Why? I had received the baptism in the
Spirit with the speaking in tongues as the Bible evidence according to Acts 2:4, and had not received the
gift of tongues according to 1 Corinthians 12. I had
received the Giver of all gifts. At some time later
when I was helping some souls to seek and receive
the baptism of the Spirit, God gave me the gift of
tongues so that I could speak at any time. I could
speak, but will not—no never! I must allow the Holy
Ghost to use the gift. It should be so, so that we shall
have divine utterances only by the Spirit. I would be
very sorry to use a gift, but the Giver has all power to
use the entire nine gifts.

I want to take you to the Scriptures to prove my
position. There are businessmen here, and they know
that in cases of law, where there are two clear witnesses they could win a case before any judge. On the
clear evidence of two witnesses any judge will give a
verdict. What has God given us? Three clear witnesses on the baptism in the Holy Spirit—more than
are necessary in law courts.

The first is in Acts 2:4, "They were all filled with
the Holy Ghost, and began to speak with other
tongues, as the Spirit gave them utterance." Here we

have the original pattern. And God gave to Peter an eternal word that couples this experience with the promise that went before: *"This is that."* And God wants you to have *that*—nothing less than *that*. He wants you to receive the baptism in the Holy Spirit according to this original Pentecostal pattern.

In Acts 10 we have another witness. Peter is in the house of Cornelius. Cornelius had had a vision of a holy angel and had sent for Peter. A person said to me one day, "You don't believe I am filled and baptized with the Holy Ghost. Why, I was ten days and ten nights on my back before the Lord and He was flooding my soul with joy." I said, "Praise the Lord, sister, that was only the beginning." The disciples were tarrying that time, and they were still, and the mighty power of God fell upon them then and the Bible tells what happened when the power fell. And that is just what happened in the house of Cornelius. The Holy Ghost fell on all them which heard the word. "And they of the circumcision which believed were astonished, as many as came with Peter, because that on the Gentiles also was poured out the gift of the Holy Ghost." What convinced these prejudiced Jews that the Holy Spirit had come? *"For they heard them speak with tongues and magnify God."* There was no other way for them to know. This evidence could not be contradicted. It is the Bible evidence.

We have heard two witnesses, and that is sufficient to satisfy the world. But God goes one better. Let us look at Acts 19:6, "And when Paul had laid his hands upon them, the Holy Ghost came on them; and they spake with tongues and prophesied." These Ephesians received the identical Bible evidence as the apostles at the beginning and they prophesied in addition. Three times the Scriptures show us this evidence of the baptism in the Spirit. I do not magnify tongues. No, by God's grace, I magnify the Giver of tongues. And I magnify above all Him whom the Holy Spirit has come to reveal to us, the Lord Jesus Christ. He it is who sends the Holy Spirit and I magnify Him because He makes no difference between us and those at the beginning.

But what are tongues for? Look at the second verse of 1 Corinthians 14 and you will see a very blessed truth. Oh, hallelujah! Have you been there, beloved? I tell you, God wants to take you there. "He that speaketh in an unknown tongue speaketh not unto men, but unto God: for no man understandeth him; howbeit in the spirit he speaketh mysteries." It goes on to say, "He that speaketh in an unknown tongue edifieth himself."

Enter into the promises of God. It is your inheritance. You will do more in one year if you are really filled with the Holy Spirit than you could do in fifty years apart from Him.

13

Concerning Spiritual Gifts

In 1 Corinthians 12:1 we read, "Now concerning spiritual gifts, brethren, I would not have you ignorant." There is a great weakness in the church of Christ because of an awful ignorance concerning the Spirit of God and the gifts He has come to bring. God would have us know His will concerning the power and manifestation of His Spirit. He would have us ever hungry to receive more and more of His Spirit. In times past I have arranged many conventions, and I have found that it is better to have a man on my platform who has not received the Baptism but who is hungry for all that God has for him. than a man who has received the Baptism and is satisfied and has settled down and become stationary and stagnant. But of course I would prefer a man that is baptized with the Holy Spirit and is still hungry for more of God. A man who is not hungry to receive more of God is out of order in any convention.

It is impossible to overestimate the importance of being filled with the Spirit. It is impossible for us to meet the conditions of the day, to walk in the light as He is in the light, to subdue kingdoms and work righteousness and bind the power of Satan unless we are filled with the Holy Spirit.

We read that in the Early Church they continued steadfastly in the apostles' doctrine and fellowship, and in breaking of bread, and in prayers. It is important for us also to continue steadfastly in these same things. For some years I was associated with a certain church group. They are very strong on the Word and are sound on water baptism; they do not neglect the breaking of bread service and have it every Lord's Day morning as they had it in the Early Church. These people seem to have everything except the match. They have the wood, but they need the fire and then they would be all ablaze. Because they lack the fire of the Holy Spirit there is no life in their meetings. One young man who attended their meetings received the Baptism with the speaking in other tongues as the Spirit gave utterance. The brethren were very upset about this and came to the father and said to him, "You must take your son aside and tell him to cease." They did not want any disturbance. The father told the son and said, "My boy, I have been attending this church for twenty years and have never seen anything of this kind. We are established in the truth and do not want anything new. We won't have it." The son replied, "If that is God's plan I will obey, but somehow or other I don't think it is." As they were going home the horse stood still; the wheels were in deep ruts. The father pulled at the reins but the horse did not move. He asked, "What do you think is up?" The son answered, "It has got established." God save us from becoming stationary.

God would have us to understand concerning spiritual gifts, and to covet earnestly the best gifts, and also to enter into the more excellent way of the fruit of the Spirit. We must beseech God for these gifts. It is a serious thing to have the Baptism and yet be stationary; to live two days in succession on the same spiritual plane is a tragedy. We must be willing to deny ourselves everything to receive the revelation of

God's truth and to receive the fullness of the Spirit. Only that will satisfy God, and nothing less must satisfy us. A young Russian received the Holy Spirit and was mightily endued with power from on High. Some sisters were anxious to know the secret of his power. The secret of his power was continuous waiting upon God. As the Holy Spirit filled him it seemed as though every breath became a prayer and so all his ministry was on an increasing line.

I know a man who was full of the Holy Spirit and would preach only when he knew that he was mightily unctionized by the power of God. He was asked to preach at a Methodist church. He was staying at the minister's house and he said, "You go on to church and I will follow." The place was packed with people and this man did not turn up and the Methodist minister, becoming anxious, sent his little girl to inquire why he did not come. As she came to the bedroom door she heard him crying out three times, "I will not go." She went back and reported that she heard the man say three times that he would not go. The minister was troubled about it, but almost immediately after this the man came in. As he preached that night, the power of God was tremendously manifested. The preacher asked him, "Why did you tell my daughter that you were not coming?" He answered, "I know when I am filled. I am an ordinary man and I told the Lord that I dared not go and would not go until He gave me a fresh filling of the Spirit. The moment the glory filled me and overflowed I came to the meeting."

Yes, there is a power, a blessing, an assurance, a rest in the presence of the Holy Spirit. You can feel His presence and know that He is with you. You need not spend an hour without this inner knowledge of

His holy presence. With His power upon you there can be no failure. You are above par all the time.

"Ye know that ye were Gentiles, carried away into these dumb idols, even as ye were led." This is the Gentile day. When the Jews refused the blessings of God He scattered them, and He has grafted the Gentiles into the olive tree where the Jews were broken off. There never has been a time when God has been so favorable to a people who were not a people. He has brought in the Gentiles to carry out His purpose of preaching the gospel to all nations and to receive the power of the Holy Spirit to accomplish this task. It is of the mercy of God that He has turned to the Gentiles and made us partakers of all the blessings that belong to the Jews; and here under this canopy of glory, because we believe, we get all the blessings of faithful Abraham.

"Wherefore I give you to understand, that no man speaking by the Spirit of God calleth Jesus accursed: and that no man can say that Jesus is the Lord, but by the Holy Ghost." There are many evil, deceiving spirits sent forth in these last days who endeavor to rob Jesus of His Lordship and of His rightful place. Many are opening the doors to these latest cults. These evil cults deny the fundamental truths of God's Word. They all deny eternal punishment and all deny the deity of Jesus Christ. You will never see the baptism of the Holy Spirit come upon a man who accepts these errors.

The all important thing is to make Jesus Lord.*

---

*"If thou shalt confess with thy mouth the Lord Jesus, and shalt believe in thine heart that God hath raised him from the dead, thou shalt be saved" (Romans 10:9).

"For to this end Christ both died and rose, and revived, that he might be Lord of both of the dead and living" (Romans 14:9).

Men can grow lopsided by emphasizing the truth of divine healing. Man can get wrong by all the time preaching on water baptism. But we never go wrong in exalting the Lord Jesus Christ, giving Him the pre-eminent place and magnifying Him as both Lord and Christ, yes, as very God of very God. As we are filled with the Holy Spirit our one desire is to magnify Him. We need to be filled with the Spirit to get the full revelation of the Lord Jesus Christ.

God's command is for us to be filled with the Spirit. We are no good if we have only a full cup; we need to have an overflowing cup all the time. It is a tragedy not to live in the fullness of overflowing. See that you never live below the overflowing tide.

"Now there are diversities of gifts, but the same Spirit"(1 Corinthians 12:4). Every manifestation of the Spirit is given that we might "profit withal." When the Holy Spirit is moving in an assembly and His gifts are in operation, everyone will receive profit. I have seen some who have been terribly switched. They believe in gifts, in prophecy, and they use these gifts apart from the power of the Holy Spirit. We must look to the Holy Spirit to show us the use of the gifts, what they are for, and when to use them, so that we may never use them without His power. I do not know of anything which is so tragic today as people using a gift without the power. Never do it. God save us from doing it.

A man who is filled with the Holy Spirit, while he may not be conscious of having any gift of the Spirit, can have the gifts made manifest through him. I have gone to many places to help and have found that under the unction of the Holy Spirit many wonderful things have happened in the midst when the glory of the Lord was upon the people. Any man who is filled with God and filled with His Spirit might at any moment have any of the nine gifts made manifest through him without knowing that he has a gift. Sometimes I have wondered whether it was better to be always full of the Holy Spirit and to see signs and wonders and miracles without any consciousness of possessing a gift or whether it was better to know one has a gift. If you have received the gifts of the Spirit and they have been blessed, you should never under any circumstances use them without the power of God upon you. Some have used the prophetic gift without the holy touch; and they have come into the realm of the natural, and it has brought ruin, caused dissatisfaction, broken hearts, upset assemblies. Do not seek the gifts unless you are purposed to abide in the Holy Spirit. They should be manifested only in the power of the Holy Spirit.

The Lord will allow you to be very drunk in His presence, but sober among people. I like to see people so filled with the Spirit that they are drunk like the 120 on the Day of Pentecost, but I don't like to see people drunk in the wrong place. That is what troubles us, somebody being drunk in a place of worship where a lot of people come in that know nothing about the Word. If you allow yourself to be drunk there, you send people away; they look at you instead of seeing God. They condemn the whole thing because you have not been sober at the right time. Paul writes, "For whether we be beside ourselves, it is to God: or whether we be sober, it is for your cause" (2 Corinthians 5:13). You can be beside yourself. You can go a bit further than being drunk. You can dance, if you will do it at the right time. So many things are commendable when all the people are in the Spirit. Many things are very foolish if the people round

about you are not in the Spirit. We must be careful
not to have a good time at the expense of somebody
else. When you have a good time you must see that
the spiritual conditions in the place lend themselves
to help you and that the people are falling in line
with you. Then you will find it always a blessing.

While it is right to covet earnestly the best gifts,
you must recognize that the all important thing is to
be filled with the power of the Holy Spirit. You will
never have trouble with people who are filled with
the power of the Holy Spirit, but you will have a lot
of trouble with people who have the gifts and have no
power. The Lord wants us to come behind in no gift,
but at the same time He wants us to be so filled with
the Holy Spirit that it will be the Holy Spirit manifesting Himself through the gifts. Where the glory of
God alone is desired you can look for every needed
gift to be made manifest. To glorify God is better
than to idolize gifts. We prefer the Spirit of God to
any gift; but we can look for the Trinity in manifestation, different gifts by the same Spirit, different ad-
ministrations but the same Lord, diversities of operation but the same God working all in all. Can you
conceive of what it will mean for our triune God to be
manifesting Himself in His fullness in our assemblies?

Watch that great locomotive boiler as it is filled
with steam. You can see the engine letting off some of
the steam as it remains stationary. It looks as though
the whole thing might burst. You can see saints like
that. They start to scream, but that is not to edification. But when the locomotive moves on, it serves the
purpose for which it was built, and pulls along much
traffic with it. It is wonderful to be filled with the
power of the Holy Spirit, and for Him to serve His
own purposes through us. Through our lips divine ut-

terances flow, our hearts rejoice and our tongue is
glad. It is an inward power within which is manifested in outward expression. Jesus Christ is glorified. As
your faith in Him is quickened, from within you there
will flow rivers of living water. The Holy Spirit will
pour through you like a great river of life and thousands will be blessed because you are a yielded channel through whom the Spirit may flow.

The most important thing, the one thing that
counts, is to see that we are filled with the Holy
Spirit, filled to overflowing. Anything less than this is
displeasing to God. We are commanded by God to be
filled with the Spirit, and in the measure you fail of
this you are that far short of the plan of God. The
Lord would have us moving on from faith to faith,
from glory to glory, from fullness to overflowing. It is
not good for us to be ever thinking in the past tense,
but we should be moving on to the place where we
dare believe God. He has declared that after the Holy
Spirit is come upon us we shall have power. I believe
there is an avalanche of power from God to be appre-
hended if we will but catch the vision.

Paul wrote at one time, "I will now come to visions
and revelations." God has put us in a place where He
expects us to have His latest revelation, the revelation
of that marvelous fact, CHRIST IN US, and what this
really means. We can apprehend Christ fully only as
we are filled and overflowing with the Spirit of God.
Our only safeguard from dropping back into our natural mind from which we can never get anything, is to
be filled and yet filled again with the Spirit of God
and to be taken on to visions and revelations on a new
line. The reason why I emphasize the importance of
the fullness of the Holy Spirit is that I want to get
you beyond all human plans and thoughts into the

fullness of vision, into the full revelation of the Lord Jesus Christ. Do you want rest? It is in Jesus. Do you want to be saved from everything the devil is bringing up in these last times? Receive and continue in the fullness of the Holy Spirit, and He will be ever revealing to you that all you need for all times is in Christ Jesus your Lord.

I desire to emphasize the importance of the Spirit's ministration and of the manifestation of the Spirit which is given to every man to profit withal. As you yield to the Spirit of the Lord He has power over your intellect, over your heart, and over your voice. The Holy Spirit has power to unveil Christ and to project the vision of Christ upon the canvas of your mind, and then He uses your tongue to glorify and magnify Him in a way that you could never do apart from the Spirit's power.

Never say that when you are filled with the Holy Spirit you are "obliged" to do this or that. When people say that they are "obliged" to do this or that, I know it is not the Spirit of God, but their own spirit moving them on to do that which is in poor taste and unprofitable. Lots of people spoil meetings because they scream. If you want to do that kind of thing, you had better get into some cellar. That is not to edification. I believe that when the Spirit of God is upon you and moving you to speak as He gives utterance, it will always be to edification. But don't spoil the prayer meeting because you go on when you should stop. Who spoils the prayer meeting? The man who starts in the Spirit and finishes in the flesh. Nothing is more lovely than prayer, but a prayer meeting is killed if you will go on and on in your own spirit when the Spirit of God is through with you. You say as you come from some meetings, "That was a lovely message if the preacher only had stopped half an hour before he did." Learn to cease immediately the unction of the Spirit lifts. The Holy Spirit is jealous. Your body is the temple, the office of the Holy Spirit, but He does not fill the temple for human glorification, but only for the glory of God. You have no license to continue beyond a "Thus saith the Lord."

There is another side to this. God would have the assembly as free as possible, and you must not put your hand upon the working of the Spirit or it will surely bring trouble. You must be prepared to allow a certain amount of extravagance in young and newly baptized souls. You must remember that when you were brought into this life of the Spirit, you had as many extravagances as anybody; but you have now become somewhat sobered down. It is a pity that some do get sobered down, for they are not where they were in the early days. We have to look to God for wisdom that we do not interfere or dampen the Spirit or quench the power of God when He is manifested in our meetings. If you want to have an assembly full of life, you must have an assembly that has the Spirit's manifestation. Few will come if there is no manifestation. We need to look to God for special grace that we do not move back to looking at things from a natural viewpoint.

The preacher, after he loses his unction, should inwardly repent and get right with God and get the unction back. We are no good without the unction of the Spirit of God. If you are filled with the grace of God, you will not be judging everybody in the assembly. You will rather be trusting everybody; you will not be frightened at what is being done; you will have a heart to believe all things and to believe that though there may be some extravagances, the Spirit of

God will take control of things and will see that the Lord Jesus Christ Himself is exalted, glorified, and revealed to hungry hearts that desire to know Him. The Lord would have us completely trust Him and become like Jesus. He wants us to dare believe God Almighty. Hallelujah!

The Holy Spirit is the One who magnifies the Lord Jesus Christ, the One who gives illumination of Him. If you are filled with the Holy Spirit, it is impossible to keep your tongue still. Talk about a dumb baptized soul! It is not to be found in the Scriptures or outside of the Scriptures. We are filled with the Spirit in order that we may magnify the Lord, and there should be no meeting in which the saints do not glorify, magnify, praise, and worship the Lord in Spirit and in truth.

I would like to give one word of caution, for failure often comes through our not recognizing the fact that we are always in the body. We will need our bodies as long as we live. But our body is to be used and controlled by the Spirit of God. We are to present our bodies, holy and acceptable unto God, which is our reasonable service. Every member of our body must be so sanctified that it works in harmony with the Spirit of God. Our very eyes must be sanctified. I desire that my eyes may be so sancitifed that they can always be used for the Lord. The Spirit of God will bring within us a compassion for souls that will be seen in our very eyes.

God has never changed the order of things. First, there comes the natural, and then the spiritual. For instance, when it is on your heart to pray, you begin in the natural and your second word will probably be under the power of the Spirit. You begin and God will end. It is the same in giving forth utterances

under the Spirit's power. You feel the moving of the
Spirit within and you begin to speak and the Spirit of
God will give forth utterance. Thousands have missed
wonderful blessings because they have not had faith
to move out and begin in the natural, in faith that the
Lord would take them into the realm of the supernatural. When you receive the Holy Spirit you receive
God's Gift, in whom are all the gifts of the Spirit. Paul
counseled Timothy to stir up the gift that was within.
You have power to stir up God's executive within you.
The way you stir up the gift within you is by beginning in faith, and then He gives forth what is needed
for the occasion. You would never begin unless you
were full of God. When we yield to timidity and fear
we simply yield to Satan. Satan whispers, "It is all
self." He is a liar. I have learned this: If the Spirit of
God is stirring me up, I have no hesitation in beginning to speak in tongues, and the Spirit of God gives
me utterance and gives me the interpretation. I find
that every time I yield to the Lord on this line I get a
divine touch; I get a leading thought from the Spirit
of God, and the meeting is moved up on the line of
faith.

Suppose you attend a meeting in faith, believing
that the Lord is going to meet you there. But perhaps
the preacher is not in harmony with God. The people
in the assembly are not getting what God wants. The
Lord knows it. He knows His people are hungry.
What happens? He will take perhaps the smallest vessels and put His power upon them. As they yield to
the Spirit they break forth in a tongue. Another yields
to the Spirit and there comes forth the interpretation.
The Lord's church has to be fed, and the Lord will
take this means of speaking to His people. Pentecostal
people cannot be satisfied with the natural message.

They are in touch with heavenly things and cannot be satisfied with anything less. They feel that when there is something lacking in a meeting, that they can look to God and He supplies that which is lacking.

When a man is filled with the Spirit, he has no conception of what he has. We are so limited in our conception of what we have received. The only way we can know the power that has been given is through the ministration and manifestation of the Spirit of God. Do you think that Peter and John knew what they had when they went up to the Temple to pray? They were limited in thought, and limited in their expression. The nearer we get to God, the more conscious we are of the poverty of the human, and we cry with Isaiah, "I am undone, I am unclean." But the Lord will bring the precious blood and the flaming coals for cleansing and refining and send us out to labor for Him, empowered by His Spirit.

God has sent forth this outpouring that we may all be brought into a revelation of our sonship—that we are sons of God, men of power, that we are to be like the Lord Jesus Christ, that we are to have the powers of sonship, the power to lay hold of that which is weak and to quicken it. The baptism of the Spirit is to make us sons of God with power. We shall be conscious of our human limits, but we shall not limit the Holy One who has come to dwell within. We must believe that since the Holy Ghost has come upon us we are indeed sons of God with power. Never say that you can't. All things are possible to them that believe. Launch out into the deep and believe that God has His all for you and that you can do all things through Him who strengthens you.

Peter and John knew that they had been in the upper room; they had felt the glory; they had been

given divine utterances. They had seen conviction on
the people. They knew that they had come into a
wonderful thing. They knew that what they had
would be ever increasing and that it would be ever
needful to cry, "Enlarge the vessel that the Holy
Spirit may have more room within." They knew that
all the old things were moved away and they had entered into an increasing and ever increasing knowledge of God, and that it was their Master's wish that
they should be filled with the Spirit of God and with
power every day and every hour. The secret of power
is the unveiling of Christ, the all-powerful One within, the revelation of God who comes to abide within
us. As they looked upon the crippled man at the
Beautiful Gate they were filled with compassion.
They were prompted by the Spirit to stop and speak
with him. They said to the lame man, "Look on us." It
was God's plan that the man should open his eyes
with expectation. Peter said, "Of silver and gold we
have none. But we have something and we will give it
to you. It is all in the name of Jesus." And then began
the ministry of God. You begin in faith and you see
what will happen. It is hidden from us at the beginning, but as we have faith in God He will come forth.
The coming forth of the power is not of us but of
God. There is no limit to what He will do. It is all in a
nutshell as you believe God. And so Peter said, "Such
as I have give I thee: In the name of Jesus Christ of
Nazareth rise up and walk." And the man who had
been in that way for forty years stood up, and began
to leap, and entered into the Temple walking and
leaping and praising God.

"For to one is given by the Spirit the word of wisdom." I want you to keep in mind the importance of
never expecting the gifts of the Spirit apart from the

power of the Spirit. In coveting the best gifts, covet to be so full of God and His glory that the gifts in manifestation will always glorify Him. We do not know all and we cannot know all that can be brought forth in the manifestation of the word of wisdom. One word of wisdom from God, one flash of light on the Word of God, is sufficient to save us from a thousand pitfalls. People have built without a word from God; they have bought things without a word from God, and they have been ensnared. They have lacked that word of wisdom which will bring them into God's plan for their lives. I have been in many places where I have needed a word of wisdom from God and this has been vouchsafed.

I will give you one instance. I am very grateful to the Lord that He has given me grace not to have a desire for money. The love of money is a great hindrance to many; and many a man is crippled in his ministry because he lets his heart run after financial matters. I was walking out one day when I met a godly man who lived near me and he said, "My wife and I have been talking together about selling our house and we feel constrained to sell it to you." As we talked together he persuaded me to buy his place, and before we said good-by I told him I would take it. We always make big mistakes when we get in a hurry. I told my wife what I had promised, and she said, "How will you manage it?" I told her that I had managed things so far, but I did not know how I was going to get through this. I somehow knew that I was out of divine order. But when a fellow gets out of divine order it seems that the last person he goes to is God. I was relying on an architect to help me, but that scheme fell through. I turned to my relatives and one after another they turned me down. I tried my friends and managed no better. My wife said to me, "Thou hast never been to God yet." What could I do?

I have a certain place in our house where I go to pray. I have been there many times. As I went I said, "Lord, if You will get me out of this scrape, I will never trouble Thee on this line again." As I waited on the Lord He just gave me one word. It seemed a ridiculous thing, but it was the wisest counsel. There is divine wisdom in every word He speaks. I came down to my wife, saying, "What do you think? The Lord has told me to go to Brother Webster." I said, "It seems very ridiculous, for he is one of the poorest men I know." He was the poorest man I knew, but he was also the richest man I knew, for he knew God. My wife said, "Do what God says, and it will be right."

I went off at once to see him, and he said as he greeted me, "Smith, what brings you so early?" I answered, "The word of God." I said to him, "About three weeks ago I promised to buy a house of a man, and I am short 100 pounds ($500). I have tried to get this money, but somehow I seem to have missed God." "How is it," he asked, "that you have come to me only now?" I answered, "Because I went to the Lord about it only last night." "Well," he said, "it is a strange thing; three weeks ago I had 100 pounds. For years I have been putting money into a cooperative system and three weeks ago I had to go and draw 100 pounds out. I hid it under the mattress. Come with me and you shall have it. Take it. I hope it will bring as great a blessing to you as it has been a trouble to me." I had had a word from God, and all my troubles were ended. This has been multiplied in a hundred ways since that time. If I had been walking along filled with the Holy Spirit, I would not have bought that house and would not have had all that anxiety. I believe the Lord wants to loose us from things of earth. But I am ever grateful for that word from God. There have been times in my life when I have been in great crises and under great weight of intercession. I have gone to meetings without the knowledge of what I would say, but somehow or other God would vouchsafe the coming forth under the power of the Spirit of some word of wisdom, just what some souls in that meeting needed. As we look to God His mind will be made known, and His revelation and His word of wisdom will be forthcoming.

14

The Word of Knowledge, and Faith

"To another the word of knowledge by the same Spirit; to another faith by the same Spirit" (1 Corinthians 12:8,9).

I believe that Satan has many devices and that they are worse today than ever before; but I also believe that there is to be a full manifestation on the earth of the power and glory of God to defeat every device of Satan.

In Ephesians 4 we are told to endeavor to keep the unity of the Spirit in the bond of peace, for there is one body, and one Spirit, one Lord, one faith, one baptism, and one God and Father of all. The baptism of the Spirit is to make us all one. Paul tells us in 1 Corinthians 12:13 that by one Spirit we are all baptized into one body, and have been all made to drink into one Spirit. It is God's thought that we speak the same thing. If we all have the full revelation of the Spirit of God we shall all see the same thing. Paul asked these Corinthians, "Is Christ divided?" When the Holy Spirit has full control, Christ is never divided, His body is not divided, there is no division. Schism and division are the products of the carnal mind.

How important it is that we shall have the manifestation of the "the word of knowledge" in our midst. The Spirit who brings forth the word of wisdom brings forth the word of knowledge. The revelation of the mysteries of God comes by the Spirit, and we must have a supernatural word of knowledge in order to convey to others the things which the Spirit of God has revealed. The Spirit of God reveals Christ in all His wonderful fullness, and He shows Him to us from the beginning to the end of the Scriptures. It is the Scriptures that make us wise unto salvation, that open to us the depths of the kingdom of heaven, which reveal all the divine mind to us.

There are thousands of people who read and study the Word of God. But it is not quickened to them. The Bible is a dead letter except by the Spirit. The Word of God can never be vital and powerful in us except by the Spirit. The words that Christ spoke were not just dead words but they were spirit and life. And so it is the thought of God that a living word, a word of truth, the word of God, a supernatural word of knowledge, shall come forth from us through the power of the Spirit of God. It is the Holy Spirit who will bring forth utterances from our lips and a divine revelation of the mind of God.

The child of God ought to thirst for the Word. "Man shall not live by bread alone, but by every word which proceedeth out of the mouth of God." It is as we feed on the Word and meditate on the message it contains, that the Spirit of God can vitalize that which we have received, and bring forth through us the word of knowledge that will be as full of power and life as when He, the Spirit of God, moved upon holy men of old and gave them these inspired Scriptures. They were all inbreathed of God as they came forth at the beginning, and through the same Spirit they should come forth from us vitalized, living, powerful and sharper than any two-edged sword.

With the gifts of the Spirit should come the fruit of

the Spirit. With wisdom we should have love, with knowledge we should have joy, and with the third gift, faith, we should have the fruit of peace. Faith is always accompanied by peace. Faith always rests. Faith laughs at impossibilities. Salvation is by faith, through grace, and it is the gift of God. We are kept by the power of God through faith. God gives faith and nothing can take it away. By faith we have power to enter into the wonderful things of God. There are three positions of faith: saving faith, which is the gift of God; the faith of the Lord Jesus; and the gift of faith. You will remember the word of the Lord Jesus Christ given to Paul, to which he refers in the 26th chapter of Acts, where the Lord commissioned him to go to the Gentiles "to open their eyes, and to turn them from darkness to light, and from the power of Satan unto God, that they may receive forgiveness of sins, and inheritance among them which are sanctified by faith that is in me."

Oh, this wonderful faith of the Lord Jesus. Your faith comes to an end. How many times I have been to the place where I have had to tell the Lord, "I have used all the faith I have," and then He has placed His own faith within me.

One of our workers said to me at Christmas time, "Wigglesworth, I never was so near the end of my purse in my life." I replied, "Thank God, you are just at the opening of God's treasures." It is when we are at the end of our own that we can enter into the riches of God's resources. It is when we possess nothing that we can possess all things.

The Lord will always meet you when you are on the line of living faith. I was in Ireland at one time and went to a house and said to the lady who came to the door, "Is Brother Wallace here?" She replied, "Oh, he has gone to Bangor, but God has sent you here for me. I need you. Come in." She told me her husband was a deacon of the Presbyterian Church. She had herself received the Baptism while she was a member of the Presbyterian Church, but they did not accept it as from God. The people of the church said to her husband, "This thing cannot go on. We don't want you to be deacon any longer, and your wife is not wanted in the church." The man was very enraged and he became incensed against his wife. It seemed as though an evil spirit possessed him, and the home that had once been peaceful became very terrible. At last he left home and left no money behind him, and the woman asked me what should she do.

We went to prayer and before we had prayed five minutes the woman was mightily filled with the Holy Spirit. I said to her, "Sit down and let me talk to you. Are you often in the Spirit like this?" She said, "Yes, and what could I do without the Holy Spirit now?" I said to her, "The situation is yours. The Word of God says that you have power to sanctify your husband. Dare to believe the Word of God. Now the first thing we must do is to pray that your husband will come back tonight." She said, "I know he won't." I said, "If we agree together, it is done." She said, "I will agree." I said to her, "When he comes home show him all possible love, lavish everything upon him. If he won't hear what you have to say, let him go to bed. The situation is yours. Get down before God and claim him for the Lord. Get into the glory just as you have got in today, and as the Spirit of God prays through you, you will find that God will grant all the desires of your heart."

A month later I saw this sister at a convention. She told how her husband came home that night and that he went to bed, but she prayed right through to victory and then laid her hands upon him. The moment she laid hands upon him he cried out for mercy. The Lord saved him and baptized him in the Holy Spirit. The power of God is beyond all our conception. The trouble is that we do not have the power of God in a full manifestation because of our finite thoughts, but as we go on and let God have His way, there is no limit to what our limitless God will do in response to a limitless faith. But you will never get anywhere except you are in constant pursuit of all the power of God.

One day when I came home from our open-air meeting I found that my wife was out. I asked, "Where is she?" I was told that she was down at Mitchell's. I had seen Mitchell that day and knew that he was at the point of death. I knew that it was impossible for him to survive the day unless the Lord undertook.

I hurried down to the house, and as I got near I heard terrible screams. I knew that something had happened. I passed Mrs. Mitchell on the staircase and asked, "What is up?" She replied, "He is gone! He is gone!" I just passed her and went into the room, and immediately I saw that Mitchell had gone. I could not understand it, but I began to pray. My wife was always afraid that I would go too far, and she laid hold of me and said, "Don't, Dad! Don't you see that he is dead?" I continued to pray and my wife continued to cry out to me, "Don't Dad. Don't you see that he is dead?" But I continued praying. I got as far as I could with my own faith, and then God laid hold of me. Oh, it was such a laying hold that I could believe for anything. The faith of the Lord Jesus laid hold of me and a solid peace came into my heart. I shouted, "He lives! He lives! He lives!" And he is living today. There is a vast difference between our faith and the faith of the Lord Jesus. The faith of the Lord Jesus is needed. We must change faith from time to time. Your faith may get to a place where it wavers. The faith of Christ never wavers. When you have that faith the thing is finished. When you have that faith you will never look at things as they are; you will see the things of nature give way to the things of the Spirit; you will see the temporal swallowed up in the eternal.

There are many who let down in sickness and do not take hold of the life of the Lord Jesus Christ that is provided for them. I was taken to see a woman who was dying and said to her, "How are things with you?" She answered, "I have faith, I believe." I said, "You know that you have not faith, you know that you are dying. It is not faith that you have, it is language." There is a difference between language and faith. I saw that she was in the hands of the devil. There was no possibility of life until he was removed from the premises. I hate the devil, and I laid hold of the woman and shouted, "Come out, you devil of death. I command you to come out in the name of Jesus." In one minute she stood on her feet in victory.

I was at a camp meeting in Cazadero, California, several years ago, and a remarkable thing happened. A man came there who was stone deaf. I prayed for him and I knew that God had healed him. Then came the test. He would always move his chair up to the platform, and every time I got up to speak he would get up as close as he could and strain his ears to catch what I had to say. The devil said, "It isn't done." I declared, "It is done." This went on for three weeks and then the manifestation came and he could hear distinctly sixty yards away. When his ears were opened he thought it was so great that he had to stop the meeting and tell everybody about it. I met him in Oakland recently and he was hearing perfectly. As we remain steadfast and unmovable on the ground of faith, we shall see what we believe for in perfect manifestation.

People say to me, "Have you not the gift of faith?" I say that it is an important gift, but what is still more important is for us every moment to be making an advancement in God. Looking at the Word of God today I find that its realities are greater to me today than they were yesterday. It is the most sublime, joyful truth that God brings an enlargement. Always an enlargement. There is nothing dead, dry or barren in this life of the Spirit; God is always moving us on to something higher, and as we move on in the Spirit our faith will always rise to the occasion as different circumstances arise.

This is how the gift of faith is manifested. You see an object and you know that your own faith is nothing in the case. The other day I was in San Francisco. I sat on a car and saw a boy in great agony on the street. I said, "Let me get out." I rushed to where the boy was. He was in agony through cramp of the stomach. I put my hands on his stomach in the name of Jesus. The boy jumped, and stared at me with astonishment. He found himself instantly free. The gift of faith dared in the face of everything. It is as we are in the Spirit that the Spirit of God will operate this gift anywhere and at any time.

When the Spirit of God is operating this gift within a man, He causes him to know what God is going to do. When the man with the withered hand was in the synagogue, Jesus got all the people to look to see what would happen. The gift of faith always knows the results. He said to the man, "Stretch forth thine hand." His word had creative force. He was not living on the line of speculation. He spoke and something happened. He spake at the beginning and the world came into being. He speaks today and these things have to come to pass. He is the Son of God and came to bring us into sonship. He was the firstfruit of the resurrection and He calls us to be firstfruits, to be the same kind of fruit.

There is an important point here. You cannot have the gifts by mere human desire. The Spirit of God distributes them severally as He will. God cannot trust some with the gift, but some who have a lowly, broken, contrite heart He can trust. One day I was in a meeting where there were many doctors and eminent men and many ministers, and the power of God fell. One humble little waitress opened her being to the Lord and was immediately filled with the Holy Spirit and began to speak in tongues. All these big men stretched their necks and looked up to see what was happening. Some were saying, "Who is it?" Then they learned it was the waitress! Nobody received but the waitress! These things are hidden and kept back from the wise and prudent, but the little children, the lowly ones, are the ones that receive. God honors the man of a broken, contrite spirit. How shall I get there? So many people want to do great things and to be seen doing them, but the one that God will use is the one that is willing to be hidden. My Lord Jesus never said He could do things, but He did them. When that funeral procession was coming up from Nain with the widow's son carried upon the bier, He stopped them. He spoke the word, "Arise!" and gave the son back to the widow. He had compassion for her. And you and I will never do anything except on the line of compassion. We shall never be able to remove the cancer until we are immersed so deeply into the power of the Holy Spirit, that the compassion of Christ is moving through us.

I find that in all my Lord did He said that He did not do it, but that another in Him did the work. What a holy submission! He was just an instrument for the glory of God. Have we reached a place where we dare to be trusted with the gift? I see in 1 Corinthians 13 that if I have faith to remove mountains and have not charity, all is a failure. When my love is so deepened in God that I only move for the glory of God, that I only seek the glory of God, then the gifts can be made manifest. God wants to be manifested and to manifest His glory to humble spirits.

A faint heart can never have a gift. There are two things essential; first, love, and second, determination, a boldness of faith that will cause God to fulfill His word. When I was baptized I had a wonderful time and had utterance in the Spirit, but for some time afterwards I did not again speak in tongues. But one day as I was helping another, the Lord again gave me utterances in the Spirit. I was one day walking along a road and speaking in tongues. There were some gardeners doing their work, and they stuck their heads out to see what was going on. I said, "Lord, you have something new for me. You said that when a man speaks in tongues, he should ask for the interpretation. I ask for the interpretation, and I'll stay right here till I get it." And from that hour the Lord gave me interpretation.

At one time I was in Lincolnshire in England and came in touch with the old pastor of an Episcopalian Church. He became much interested and asked me

into his library. I never heard anything sweeter than
the prayer the old man uttered as he got down to
pray. He began to pray, "Lord, make me holy. Lord,
sanctify me." I called out, "Wake up! Wake up now!
Get up and sit in your chair." He sat up and looked at
me. I said to him, "I thought you were holy." He answered, "Yes." "Then what makes you ask God to do
what He has done for you?" He began to laugh and
then to speak in tongues. Let us move into the realm
of faith, and live in the realm of faith, and let God
have His way.

15

Gifts of Healings and Miracles

God has given us much in these last days; and where much is given, much will be required. The Lord has said to us, "Ye are the salt of the earth: but if the salt have lost his savour, wherewith shall it be salted? it is thenceforth good for nothing, but to be cast out, and to be trodden under foot of men" (Matthew 5:13). We see a thought on the same line when our Lord Jesus says, "If a man abide not in me, he is cast forth as a branch, and is withered; and men gather them, and cast them into the fire, and they are burned"; and then He adds, "If ye abide in me, and my words abide in you, ye shall ask what ye will, and it shall be done unto you" (John 15:6,7). If we do not move on with the Lord and do not walk in the light of revealed truth, we shall become as the savorless salt, as a withered branch. We must forget those things that are behind, the past failures and the past blessings; we must reach forth for those things which are before, and press toward the mark for the prize of our high calling of God in Christ Jesus.

For many years the Lord has been moving me on and keeping me from spiritual stagnation. I was in a certain church and I was sure I was saved and was sure I was all right. The Lord said to me, "Come out," and I came out. When I was with another group I was sure I was all right now. But the Lord said, "Come out." Then I went into a third church. At that time it was full of life and there were revivals everywhere. But it went into natural things and the great revivals that they had in those early days ceased. The Lord said to me, "Come out," and I came out. I have had to come out three times since. I believe that this Pentecostal revival that we are now in is the best thing that the Lord has on the earth today, and yet I believe that God has something that is going to be better. God has no use for any man who is not hungering and thirsting for yet more of Him and His righteousness.

The Lord has told us to covet earnestly the best gifts, and we need to be covetous for those that will bring Him most glory. We need to see the gifts of healing and the working of miracles in operation today. Some say that it is necessary for us to have the gift of discerning of spirits in operation with the gifts of healing, but even apart from this gift I believe the Holy Spirit will have a divine revelation for us as we deal with the sick. Most people seem to have discernment, or think they have, and if they would turn it on themselves for twelve months they would never want to discern again. The gift of discerning of spirits is not criticism. I am satisfied that in Pentecostal circles today our paramount need is more perfect love.

Perfect love will never want the preeminence in everything; it will never want to take the place of another; it will always be willing to take the back seat. At conventions there is always someone who wants to give a message, who wants to be heard. If you have a desire to go to a convention you should have three things settled in your mind. Do I want to be heard? Do I want to be seen? Do I want financial gain? If I have these things in my heart I have no right to be there. The one thing that must move us must be the

constraining love of God to minister for Him. A
preacher always loses out when he gets his mind on
finances. It is well for Pentecostal preachers to avoid
making much of finances except to stir up people to
help our missionaries. A preacher who gets big collec-
tions for the missionaries need never fear; the Lord
will take care of his finances. A preacher should not
land at a place and say that God had sent him. I am
always fearful when I hear a man advertising this. If
he is sent of God, the saints will know it. God has His
plans for His servants and we must so live in His
plans that He will place us where He wants us. If you
seek nothing but the will of God, He will always put
you in the right place at the right time. I want you to
see that the gifts of healing and the working of miracles are part of the Spirit's plan and will come forth in
operation as we are working along that plan. I must
know the movement of the Spirit and the voice of
God. I must understand the will of God if I am to see
the gifts of the Spirit in operation.

The gifts of healing are so varied. You may talk
with ten people and every case be different. I am
never happier in the Lord than when I am in a bedroom with a sick person. I have had more revelations
of the Lord's presence when I have ministered to the
sick at their bedsides than at any other time. It is as
your heart goes out to the needy ones in deep compassion that the Lord manifests His presence. You are
able to locate their position. It is then that you know
that you must be filled with the Spirit to deal with the
conditions before you.

Where people are in sickness you find frequently
that they are dense about the Bible. They usually
know three verses though. They know about Paul's
thorn in the flesh, and that Paul told Timothy to take

a little wine for his stomach's sake, and that Paul left someone sick somewhere; they forget his name, and don't remember the name of the place, and don't know where the chapter is. Most people think they have a thorn in the flesh. The chief thing in dealing with a person who is sick is to ascertain their exact position. As you are ministering under the Spirit's power the Lord will let you see just that which will be more helpful and most faith-inspiring to them.

When I was in the plumbing business I enjoyed praying for the sick. Urgent calls would come and I would have no time to wash, and with my hands all black I would preach to these sick ones, my heart all aglow with love. Ah, you must have your heart in the thing when you pray for the sick. You have to get right to the bottom of the cancer with a divine compassion and then you will see the gifts of the Spirit in operation.

I was called at ten o'clock one night to pray for a young woman who was given up by the doctor and who was dying of consumption. As I looked, I saw that unless God undertook it was impossible for her to live. I turned to the mother and said, "Well, mother, you will have to go to bed." She said, "Oh, I have not had my clothes off for three weeks." I said to the daughters, "You will have to go to bed," but they did not want to go. It was the same with the son. I put on my overcoat and said, "Good-bye, I'm off." They said, "Oh, don't leave us." I said, "I can do nothing here." They said, "Oh, if you will stop, we will all go to bed." I knew that God would move nothing in an atmosphere of mere natural sympathy and unbelief.

They all went to bed and I stayed, and that was surely a time as I knelt by that bed, face to face with death and with the devil. But God can change the hardest situation and make you know that He is almighty.

Then the fight came. It seemed as though the heavens were brass. I prayed from eleven to three-thirty in the morning. I saw the glimmering light on the face of the sufferer and saw her pass away. The devil said, "Now you are done for. You have come from Bradford and the girl has died on your hands." I said, "It can't be. God did not send me here for nothing. This is a time to change strength." I remembered that passage which said, "Men ought always to pray and not to faint." Death had taken place, but I knew that my God was all powerful and He that had split the Red Sea is just the same today. It was a time when I would not have no, and God said yes. I looked at the window and at that moment the face of Jesus appeared. It seemed as though a million rays of light were coming from His face. As He looked at the one who had just passed away, the color came back to the face. She rolled over and fell asleep. Then I had a glorious time. In the morning she woke early, put on a dressing gown and walked to the piano. She started to play and to sing a wonderful song. The mother and the sister and the brother came down to listen. The Lord had undertaken. A miracle had been wrought.

The Lord is calling us along this way. I am thanking God for difficult cases. The Lord has called us into heart union with Himself; He wants His bride to have one heart and one Spirit with Him and to do what He Himself loved to do. That case had to be a miracle. The lungs were gone, they were just in shreds, but the Lord restored lungs that were perfectly sound.

There is a fruit of the Spirit that must accompany the gift of healing, and that is longsuffering. The man who is going through with God, to be used in healing must be a man of longsuffering. He must be always ready with a word of comfort. If the sick one is in dis-

tress and helpless and does not see everything eye to
eye with you, you must bear with him. Our Lord
Jesus Christ was filled with compassion and lived and
moved in a place of longsuffering, and we will have to
get into this place if we are to help needy ones.

There are some times when you pray for the sick
and you are apparently rough. But you are not dealing with a person, you are dealing with the Satanic
forces that are binding the person. Your heart is full
of love and compassion to all, but you are moved to a
holy anger as you see the place the devil has taken in
the body of the sick one, and you deal with his position with a real forcefulness. One day a pet dog fol-
lowed a lady out of her house and ran all round her
feet. She said to the dog, "My dear, I cannot have you
with me today." The dog wagged its tail and made a
big fuss. She said, "Go home, my dear." But the dog
did not go. At last she shouted roughly, "Go home,"
and off it went. Some people deal with the devil like
that. The devil can stand all the comfort you like to
give him. Cast him out! You are dealing not with the
person, you are dealing with the devil. Demon power
must be dislodged in the name of the Lord. You are
always right when you dare to deal with sickness as
with the devil. Much sickness is caused by some miscon-
duct; there is something wrong; there is some neglect
somewhere, and Satan has had a chance to get in. It is
necessary to repent and confess where you have given
place to the devil, and then he can be dealt with.

When you deal with a cancer case, recognize that it
is a living evil spirit that is destroying the body. I
prayed for a woman in Los Angeles who was suffering with cancer, and as soon as it was cursed it
stopped bleeding. It was dead. The next thing that
happened was that the natural body pressed it out be-

cause the natural body had no room for dead matter. It came out like a great big ball with tens of thousands of fibers. All these fibers had been pressing into the flesh. These evil powers move to get further hold of the system, but the moment they are destroyed their hold is gone. Jesus said to His disciples that He gave them power to loose and power to bind. It is our privilege in the power of the Holy Spirit to loose the prisoners of Satan and to let the oppressed go free.

Take your position from the First Epistle of John and declare, "Greater is He that is in me than he that is in the world." Then recognize that it is not you that has to deal with the power of the devil, but the Greater One that is in you. Oh, what it means to be filled with Him. You can do nothing of yourself, but He that is in you will win the victory. Your being has become the temple of the Spirit. Your mouth, your mind, your whole being becomes exercised and worked upon by the Spirit of God.

I was called to a certain town in Norway. The hall seated about 1500 people. When I got to the place it was packed, and hundreds were trying to get in. There were some policemen there. The first thing I did was to preach to the people outside the building. Then I said to the policemen, "It hurts me very much that there are more people outside than inside and I feel I must preach to the people. I would like you to get me the market place to preach in." They secured for me a great park and a big stand was erected, and I was able to preach to thousands. After the preaching we had some wonderful cases of healing. One man came a hundred miles, bringing his food with him. He had not been passing anything through his stomach for over a month as he had a great cancer on his stomach. He was healed at that meeting, and opening his parcel, he began eating before all the people. There was a young woman there with a stiff hand. Instead of the mother making the child use her arm she had allowed the child to keep the arm dormant until it was stiff, and she had grown up to be a young woman and was like the woman that was bowed down with the spirit of infirmity. As she stood before me I cursed the spirit of infirmity in the name of Jesus. It was instantly cast out and the arm was free. Then she waved it all over. At the close of the meeting the devil laid out two people with fits. When the devil is manifesting himself, then is the time to deal with him. Both of these people were delivered, and when they stood up and thanked and praised the Lord, what a wonderful time we had.

We need to wake up and to believe God. Before God could bring me to this place He broke me a thousand times. I have wept, I have groaned, I have travailed many a night until God broke me. It seems to me that until God has mowed you down you never can have this longsuffering for others. We can have the gifts of healing and the working of miracles in operation only as we stand in the divine power that God gives us. We stand believing God, and having done all we still stand believing.

We have been seeing wonderful miracles these last days and they are only a little of what we are going to see. I believe that we are right on the threshold of wonderful things, but I want to emphasize that all these things will be through the power of the Holy Spirit. You must not think that these gifts will fall upon you like ripe cherries. There is a sense in which you have to pay the price for everything you get. We must covet God's best gifts, and say Amen to any preparation the Lord takes us through so we may be humble, usable vessels through whom He can operate by means of the Spirit's power.

16

The Gift of Prophecy

In 1 Corinthians 12:10, speaking of the diversities of
gifts by the same Spirit, Paul writes, "To another
prophecy." We see the importance of this gift from 1
Corinthians 14:1, where we are told to follow after
charity and desire spiritual gifts, but rather that we
may prophesy. We see also that he that prophesieth
speaketh unto man to edification and exhortation and
comfort. How important it is then that we should
have this gift in manifestation in the church in order
that the saints might be built up and made strong and
receive the comfort of God. But with this as all other
gifts we should see that it is operated by the Spirit's
power and brought forth in the unction of the Spirit
so that everyone who shall hear prophecy, as it is
brought forth by the Spirit of God, shall know that it is
God who is bringing forth that which is for the edification of those who hear. It is the Spirit of God who takes
the deep things of God and reveals them, and it is He
who unctionizes the prophet to give forth that which
is a revelation of the things of God.

Utterance in prophecy has a real lifting power and
gives real light on the truth to those who hear. Prophecy is never a mind reflection; it is something far
deeper than this. By means of prophecy we receive
that which is the mind of the Lord; and as we receive
these blessed, fresh utterances through the Spirit of
the Lord the whole assembly is lifted into the realm

of the spiritual. Our hearts and minds and whole bodies receive a quickening through the Spirit-given word. As the Spirit brings forth prophecy we find there is healing and salvation and power. For this reason it is one of the gifts that we ought to covet.

While we appreciate true prophecy, we must not forget that the Scriptures warn us in no uncertain manner concerning that which is false. In 1 John 4:1 we are told, "Beloved, believe not every spirit, but try the spirits whether they are of God: because many false prophets are gone out into the world." And John tells us how we can tell the difference between the true and the false, "Hereby know ye the Spirit of God: Every spirit that confesseth that Jesus Christ is come in the flesh is of God: and every spirit that confesseth not that Jesus Christ is come in the flesh is not of God: but this is that spirit of antichrist, whereof ye have heard that it should come." There are voices which seem like prophecy. Some people have fallen into terrible darkness and bondage through listening to these counterfeits of the true gift of prophecy. True prophecy is always Christ-exalting, magnifying the Son of God, exalting the blood of Jesus Christ, encouraging the saints to praise and worship the true God. False prophecy deals with things that do not edify and is designed to puff up its hearers and to lead them into error.

Many picture Satan as a great, ugly monster with great ears, eyes and a tail; but the Scriptures give us no such picture of him. He was a being of great beauty whose heart became lifted up. He is manifesting himself everywhere today as an angel of light. He is full of pride; and if you don't watch, he will try to make you think you are somebody. This is the weakness of most preachers and most men—the idea of

being somebody! There are none of us who are anything; and the more we know we are nothing, the
more God can make us a channel of His power. May
the dear Lord save us from the things that cause us to
be proud—they are the devil's traps. True prophecy
will show you that Christ is all in all and that you are
in yourself less than nothing and vanity. False prophecy will not magnify Christ but will make you think
that after all you are going to be some great one. You
may be sure that such is inspired by "the chief of the
sons of pride."

I want to warn you against the foolishness of listening for voices. Look in the Bible. Here we have the
voice of God who at sundry times and in divers man-
ners, spake in time past unto the fathers by the prophets, and hath in these last days spoken unto us by
His Son. Don't run away with anything else. If you
hear the voice of God, it will be on the line of the
Scriptures of truth given in the inspired Word. In Revelation 22:18,19 we see the danger of attempting to
add to or take from the prophecy of this Book. True
prophecy, as it comes forth in the power of the Spirit
of God, will neither take from nor add to the Scriptures, but will intensify and quicken that which already has been given to us of God. The Holy Spirit
will bring to our remembrance all the things that
Jesus said and did. True prophecy will bring forth
things new and old out of the Scriptures of truth and
will make them living and powerful to us.

Some may ask, "If we have the Scriptures, why do
we need prophecy?" The Scriptures themselves answer this question. God has said that in the last days
He will pour out of His Spirit upon all flesh, "and
your sons and your daughters shall prophesy." The
Lord knew that in these last days prophecy would be

a real means of blessing to us, and that is why we can count on Him giving us, by means of the Spirit, through His servants and His handmaids, true prophetic messages.

I was at a meeting in Scotland and came in touch with two young women who were in a great state of excitement. These two girls were telegraph operators and were precious young women, having received the baptism in the Spirit. They both longed to be missionaries. But whatever our spiritual state is we are subject to temptations. An evil power came to one of these young women and said, "If you will obey me, I will make you one of the most wonderful missionaries that ever went out." This was just the devil or one of his agents acting as an angel of light. One of these young women was captured immediately and she became so excited that her sister saw there was something wrong and asked the superintendent to allow them to be free for a time.

As she went into a room, Satan, endeavoring to imitate the Spirit of God, manifested himself in a voice, and led this young woman to believe that the missionary enterprise would be unfolded that night if she would obey. This evil spirit said, "Don't tell anybody but your sister." I reckon that everything of God can be told everybody. If you cannot preach what you live, your life is wrong. Some day it will be told from the housetop. Don't think you will get out of it. That which is pure cometh to the light. He that doeth truth cometh to the light that his deeds may be made manifest, that they are wrought in God.

The evil power went on to say to this girl, "You go to the railroad station tonight, and there will be a train coming in at 7:32. Buy a ticket for yourself and your sister. Then you will have six pence left. You will find a woman in a carriage dressed as a nurse, and opposite her will be a gentlemen who has all the money you need." She bought her ticket and had just six pence left. The first thing came right. Next, the train came in at exactly 7:32. But the next thing did not come. They ran from the top to the bottom of that railroad train before it moved out and nothing turned out as they had been told. As soon as the train moved out the same voice came and said, "Over on the other platform." All that night until 9:30 these two young women were rushed from platform to platform. As soon as it was 9:30 this same evil power said, "Now that I know you will obey me, I will make you the greatest missionaries." Always something big! They might have known it was all wrong. This evil power said, "This gentleman will take you to a certain bank at a certain corner in Glasgow where he will put all that money in for you." Banks are not open at that time of night in Glasgow. If she had gone to the street this evil spirit mentioned, there probably would not have been a bank there. All they needed was a little common sense and they would have seen that it was not the Lord. If you have your heart open for these kind of voices you will soon get into a trap. We must ever remember that there are many evil spirits in the world.

Were these two people delivered? Yes, after much travail with God, they were completely delivered. Their eyes were opened to see that this thing was not of God but of the devil. These two sisters are now laboring for the Lord in China and doing a blessed work for Him. If you do get into error on these lines, praise God there is a way out. I praise God that He will break us down till all pride leaves us.

Paul wrote at the commandment of the Lord, "Let

the prophets speak two or three, and let the others judge. If anything be revealed to another that sitteth by, let the first hold his peace. For ye may all prophesy one by one, that all may learn, and all may be comforted" (1 Corinthians 14:29-31). If you are not humble enough to allow your prophecy to be judged, it is as surely wrong as you are wrong. Prophecy has to be judged. A meeting such as this one that Paul suggests would certainly be the greatest meeting you ever had. Praise God, the tide will rise to this. It will all come into perfect order when the church is bathed and lost in the great ideal of only glorifying Jesus. Then things will come to pass that will be worthwhile.

Coupled with prophecy you will have goodness, the fruit of the Spirit. They were holy men who spoke in prophecy in days of old as the Holy Spirit prompted them, and so today the prophet who can be trusted is a man that is full of goodness, that goodness which is the fruit of the Spirit. But when he gets out of this position and depends on his own personality, he is in danger of being puffed up and becoming an instrument for the enemy.

I knew some people who had a wonderful farm, very productive, in a very good neighborhood. They listened to voices telling them to sell everything and go to Africa. These voices so unhinged them that they had scarcely had time to sell out. They sold their property at a ridiculous price. The same voices told them of a certain ship they were to sail on, but when they got to the port they found there wasn't a ship by that name. The difficulty was to get them not to believe these false voices. They said perhaps it was the mind of the Lord to give them another ship, and the voice soon gave them the name of another ship. When they reached Africa they knew no language that was spoken there. But the voice did not let them stop. They had to come back, brokenhearted, shaken through, and having lost all confidence in everything. If these people had had sense to go to some men of God who were filled with the Spirit and seek their counsel, they would soon have been persuaded that these voices were not of God. But listening to these voices always brings about a spiritual pride that makes a man or woman think that they are superior to their brethren and that they are above taking counsel of men who they think are not so filled with the Spirit as they are. If you hear any voices that make you think that you are superior to those whom God has put in the church to rule the church, watch out; that is surely the devil.

We read in the Revelation that the testimony of Jesus is the spirit of prophecy. You will find that true prophetic utterance always exalts the Lamb of God.

No prophetic touch is of any good unless there is fire in it. I never expect to be used of God till the fire burns. I feel that if I ever speak, it must be by the Spirit. At the same time remember that the prophet must prophesy according to the measure of faith. If you rise up in your weakness—but rise up in love because you want to honor God—and just begin, you will find the presence of the Lord upon you. Act in faith and the Lord will meet you.

May God take us on and on into this glorious fact of faith, that we may be so directed by the Holy Spirit that God will work through us on the line of the miraculous and on the lines of prophecy where we shall always know that it is no longer we but He who is working through us, bringing forth that which is in His own divine good pleasure.

17

The Discerning of Spirits

"To another discerning of spirits" (1 Corinthians 12:10). There is a vast difference between natural and spiritual discernment. When it comes to natural discernment you will find many people loaded with it, and they can see so many faults in others. To such the words of Christ in the sixth chapter of Luke surely apply, "Why beholdest thou the mote that is in thy brother's eye, but perceivest not the beam that is in thine own eye?" If you want to manifest natural discernment, focus the same on yourself for at least twelve months and you will see so many faults in yourself that you will never want to fuss about the faults of another. In the sixth chapter of Isaiah we read of the prophet being in the presence of God, and he found that even his lips were unclean and everything was unclean. But praise God, there is the same live coal for us today, the baptism of fire, the perfecting of the heart, the purifying of the mind, the regeneration of the spirit. How important it is that the fire of God shall touch our tongues.

In 1 John 4:1 we are told, "Beloved, believe not every spirit, but try the spirits whether they are of God." We are further told, "And every spirit that confesseth not that Jesus Christ is come in the flesh is not of God: and this is that spirit of antichrist, whereof ye have heard that it should come; and even now already is it in the world" (1 John 4:3). From time to time as

I have seen a person under the power of evil, I have said to the power of evil, or Satanic force that is within the possessed person, "Did Jesus Christ come in the flesh?" and straightway they have answered, "No." They either say, "No," or hold their tongues, refusing altogether to acknowledge that the Lord Jesus Christ came in the flesh. It is then, remembering that further statement of John's, "Greater is he that is in you than he that is in the world," that you can in the name of the Lord Jesus Christ deal with the evil powers and command them to come out. We as Pentecostal people must know the tactics of the evil one and must be able to displace and dislodge him from his position.

I was preaching in Doncaster, England, at one time on the line of faith and a number of people were delivered. There was a man present who was greatly interested and moved by what he saw. He was suffering himself with a stiff knee and had flannel wound around it. After he got home he said to his wife, "I have taken in Wigglesworth's message, and now I am going to act on it and get deliverance. Wife, I want you to be the audience." He took hold of his knee and said, "Come out, you devil, in the name of Jesus." Then he said, "It is all right, wife." He took the flannel off and found he was all right without the bandage. The next night he went to the little Primitive Methodist Church where he worshiped. There were in the church a lot of young people who were sick and the man had a tremendous time delivering his friends through the name of Jesus. He had been given to see that a great many ills to which flesh is heir are nothing else but the operation of the enemy, but his faith had risen and he saw that in the name of Jesus there was a power that was more than a match for the enemy.

I arrived one night at Gottenberg in Sweden and was asked to hold a meeting there. In the midst of the meeting a man fell full length in the doorway. The evil spirit threw him down, manifesting itself and disturbing the whole meeting. I rushed to the door and laid hold of this man and cried out to the evil spirit within him, "Come out, you devil! In the name of Jesus we cast you out as an evil spirit." I lifted him up and said, "Stand on your feet and walk in the name of Jesus." I don't know whether anybody in the meeting understood me except the interpreter, but the devils knew what I said. I talked in English but these devils in Sweden cleared out. A similar thing happened in Christiania.

The devil will endeavor to fascinate through the eyes and through the mind. At one time there was brought to me a beautiful young woman who had fallen in love with a preacher; and just because he did not marry her, the devil took advantage and made her fanatical and mad. They brought her 250 miles in that condition. She had previously received the baptism in the Spirit. You ask, "Is there any place for the enemy in one that has been baptized in the Holy Spirit?" Our only safety is in going on with God and in constantly being filled with the Holy Spirit. You must not forget Demas. He must have been baptized with the Holy Spirit, for he appears to have been a right-hand worker with Paul; but the enemy got him to the place where he loved this present world and he dropped off. When they brought this young woman to me the evil power was immediately discerned and immediately I cast the thing out in the name of Jesus. It was a great joy to present her before all the people in her right mind again.

There is a life of perfect deliverance, and this is

where God wants you to be. If I find my peace is disturbed on any line, I know it is the enemy who is trying to work. How do I know this? Because the Lord has promised to keep your mind in perfect peace when it is stayed on Him. Paul tells us to present our bodies a living sacrifice, holy, acceptable unto God, which is our reasonable service; the Holy Spirit breathes through him, "And be not conformed to this world; but be ye transformed by the renewing of your mind, that ye may prove what is that good, and acceptable, and perfect will of God" (Romans 12:2). He further tells us in Philippians 4:8, "Finally, brethren, whatsoever things are true, whatsoever things are honest, whatsoever things are just, whatsoever things are pure, whatsoever things are lovely, whatsoever things are of good report; if there be any virtue, and if there be any praise, think on these things." As we think about that which is pure, we become pure. As we think about that which is holy, we become holy. And as we think about our Lord Jesus Christ, we become like Him. We are changed into the likeness of the object on which our gaze is fixed.

To discern spirits we must dwell with Him who is holy, and He will give the revelation and unveil the mask of Satanic power on all lines. In Australia I went to one place where there were disrupted and broken homes. The people were so deluded by the evil power of Satan that men had left their wives, and wives had left their husbands. That is the devil! May God deliver us from such evils in these days. There is no one better than the companion God has given you. I have seen so many broken hearts and so many homes that have been wrecked. We need a real revelation of these evil seducing spirits which come in and fascinate by the eye and destroy lives and bring the work of God into disrepute. But there is always flesh behind it. It is never clean; it is unholy, impure, Satanic, devilish, and hell is behind it. If the enemy comes in to tempt you on any line like this, I beseech you to look instantly to the Lord Jesus. He can deliver you from any such Satanic power. You must be separated on all lines if you are going to have faith.

The Holy Spirit will give us this gift of discerning of spirits if we desire it so that we may perceive by revelation this evil power which comes in to destroy. We can reach out and get this unction of the Spirit that will reveal these things unto us.

You will have people come to meetings who are spiritists. You must be able to deal with spiritist conditions. You can so deal with them that they will not have any power in the meetings. If you ever have Theosophists or Christian Scientists, you must be able to discern them and take care of them. Never play with them; always clear them out. They are better with their own company always, unless they are willing to be delivered from the delusion they are in. Remember the warning of the Lord Jesus, "The thief cometh not, but for to steal, and to kill, and to destroy."

Before Satan and his evil spirits can enter, there has to be an open door. Hear what the Scriptures say: "That wicked one toucheth him not" (1 John 5:18). "The Lord shall preserve thee from all evil: He shall perserve thy soul" (Psalm 121:7). How does Satan get an opening? When the saint ceases to seek after holiness, purity, righteousness, truth; when he ceases to pray, stops reading the Word and gives way to carnal appetites, then it is that Satan comes. So often sickness comes as a result of disobedience. David said, "Before I was afflicted, I went astray." Seek the Lord and He will sanctify every thought, every act, till your whole being is ablaze with holy purity and your one desire will be for Him who has created you in holiness. Oh, this holiness! Can we be made pure? We can. Every inbred sin must go. God can cleanse away every evil thought. Can we have a hatred for sin and a love for righteousness? Yes, God will create within thee a pure heart. He will take away the stony heart out of the flesh. He will sprinkle thee with clean water and thou shalt be cleansed from all thy filthiness. When will He do it? When you seek Him for such inward purity.

18

The Gift of Tongues

"Follow after charity, and desire spiritual gifts, but rather that ye may prophesy. For he that speaketh in an unknown tongue, speaketh not unto men, but unto God: for no man understandeth him; howbeit in the spirit he speaketh mysteries" (1 Corinthians 14:1,2).

It is necessary that we have a great desire for spiritual gifts. We must thirst after them and covet them earnestly because the gifts are necessary and important. Then, we by the grace of God having received the gifts, may be used for God's glory.

God has ordained this speaking in an unknown tongue unto Himself as a wonderful, supernatural means of communication in the Spirit. As we speak to Him in the unknown tongue we speak wonderful mysteries in the Spirit. In Romans 8:27 we read, "He that searcheth the hearts knoweth what is the mind of the Spirit, because he maketh intercession for the saints according to the will of God." Many times as we speak unto God in an unknown tongue we are in intercession and as we pray thus in the Spirit we pray according to the will of God. And there is such a thing as the Spirit making intercession with groanings which cannot be uttered.

On this line I want to tell you about Willie Burton, who is laboring for God in the Belgian Congo. Brother Burton is a mighty man of God and is giving his life for the heathen in Africa. He took fever and went down to death. They said, "He has preached his last; what shall we do?" All their hopes seemed to be blighted; and there they stood with broken hearts wondering what was going to take place. They left him for dead; but in a moment, without any signal, he stood right in the midst of them; and they could not understand it. The explanation he gave was that when he came to himself, he realized a warmth going right through his body; and there wasn't one thing wrong with him. How did it come about? It was a mystery until he went to London and was telling the people how he was left for dead and then was raised up. A lady came up and asked for a private conversation with him. She asked, "Do you keep a diary?" He answered, "Yes." She told him, "It happened on a certain day that I went to pray; and as soon as I knelt, I had you on my mind. The Spirit of the Lord took hold of me and prayed through me in an unknown tongue. A vision came before me in which I saw you laid out helpless; and I cried out in the unknown tongue till I saw you rise up and go out of that room." She had kept a note of the time and when he turned to his diary he found that it was exactly the time when he was raised up.

There are great possibilities as we yield to the Spirit and speak unto God in quiet hours. God wants you to be filled with the Holy Spirit so that everything about you shall be charged with the dynamic of heaven.

"He that speaketh in an unknown tongue edifieth himself; but he that prophesieth edifieth the church" (1 Corinthians 14:4). I want you to see that he that speaketh in an unknown tongue edifieth himself or builds himself up. We must be edified before we can edify the church. I cannot estimate what I, personally, owe to the Holy Spirit method of spiritual edification. I am one of the biggest conundrums in the world. There never was a weaker man on the platform. Language? None. Inability—full of it. All natural things in my life point exactly opposite to my being able to stand on the platform and preach the gospel. The secret is that the Holy Spirit came and brought this wonderful edification of the Spirit. I had been reading this Word continually as well as I could, but the Holy Spirit came and took hold of it—for the Holy Ghost is the breath of it—and He illuminated it to me. And He gives me language that I cannot speak fast enough; it comes too fast; and it is there because God has given it. When the Comforter is come He shall teach you All things; and He has given me this supernatural means of speaking in an unkown tongue to edify myself, so that, after being edified, I can edify the church.

In 1 John 2:20 we read, "But ye have an unction from the Holy One, and ye know all things." In verse 27 we read, "But the anointing which ye have received of him abideth in you, and ye need not that any man teach you: but as the same anointing teacheth you of all things, and is truth, and is no lie, and even as it hath taught you, ye shall abide in him." Even, when you are baptized in the Spirit you may say, "I seem so dry, I don't know where I am." The Word says you have an unction. Thank God you have received an anointing. The Holy Spirit here says that He is abiding and that He teaches you of all things. These are great and definite positions for you. The Holy Spirit would have you stir up your faith to believe that this word is true, that you have the unction and that the anointing abideth. As you rise up in the morning, believe this wonderful truth; and as you yield to the Spirit's presence and power you will find yourself speaking unto God in the Spirit, and you will find that you are personally being edified by doing this. Let everything about you be a lie, but let this Word of God be true. The devil will say you are the driest person and that you will never do anything, but you believe God's Word that the anointing which ye have received of Him abideth in you.

"I would that ye all spake with tongues, but rather that ye prophesied: for greater is he that prophesieth than he that speaketh with tongues, except he interpret, that the church may receive edification" (1 Corinthians 14:5). You must understand that God would always have you to be ready for a prophecy, for everyone who has received the Holy Spirit has a right to prophesy. In verse 31 of 1 Corinthians 14 we read, "Ye may all prophesy one by one." Now prophecy is far in advance of speaking in tongues, except that you have the interpretation of the speaking in tongues; then God gets an equivalent to prophecy. In verse 13 we read, "Let him that speaketh in an unknown tongue pray that he may interpret." This is an important word.

After receiving the baptism in the Holy Spirit and speaking in tongues as the Spirit gave utterance, I did not speak with tongues again for nine months. I was troubled about it because I was in many meetings laying hands on people that they might receive the Holy Spirit, and they were speaking in tongues; but I did not have the joy of speaking myself. God wanted to show me that the speaking in tongues as the Spirit gave utterance, which I received when I received the Baptism, was distinct from the gift of tongues which I subsequently received. When I laid hands on other people and they received the Holy Spirit, I used to think, "Oh, Lord Jesus, it would be nice if You would let me speak." He withheld the gift from me, for He knew that I would meet many who would say that the baptism of the Holy Spirit can be received without the speaking in tongues, and that people simply received the gift of tongues when they received the Baptism. I did not receive the gift of tongues at that time, but nine months later I was going out of the door one morning, speaking to the Lord in my own heart, when there came a volume of tongues. When the tongues stopped, I said to the Lord, "Now, Lord, I did not do it, and I wasn't seeking it; so You have done it, and I am not going to move from this place until you give me interpretation." And then came an interpretation which has been fulfilled all the world over. Is it the Holy Spirit who speaks? Then the Holy Spirit can interpret. Let him that speaks in a tongue pray that he may interpret, and God will give it. We must not rush through without getting a clear understanding of what God has to say to us.

"What is it then? I will pray with the spirit, and I will pray with the understanding also: I will sing with the spirit, and I will sing with the understanding also" (1 Corinthians 14:15). If you pray in an unknown tongue in the Spirit, you do not know what you are praying; you have no understanding of it. It is unfruitful to those round about you; but you have the same power to pray with the understanding under the unction of the Spirit as you have to pray in an unknown tongue. Some say, "Oh, I could do that, but it would be myself doing it." If YOU pray, it is yourself, and everything you do in the beginning is yourself. I kneel down to pray and the first and second sentences may be in the natural; but as soon as *I* have finished, the Spirit begins to pray through me. The first may be yourself. Granted. The next will be the Holy Spirit and He will take you through; praise the Lord. Everything but faith will say, "That isn't right." Faith says, "It is right." The natural man says, "It isn't right." Faith says, "It is right." Paul says, "I will pray with the spirit, and I will pray with the understanding also"; and he does it in faith. The devil is against it and your own self-life is against it. May God the Holy Spirit bring us into the blessed place where we may live, walk, pray and sing in the Spirit, and pray and sing with the understanding also. Faith will do it. Faith has a deaf ear to the devil and to the working of the natural mind, and a big ear to God. Faith has a deaf ear to yourself and an open ear to God. Faith won't take any notice of feelings. Faith says, "You are complete in Him."

It is a wonderful thing to pray in the Spirit and to sing in the Spirit, praying in tongues and singing in tongues as the Spirit of God gives you utterance. I never get out of bed in the morning without having communion with God in the Spirit. It is the most wonderful thing on earth. It is most lovely to be in the Spirit. You begin the day like that and you will be conscious of the guidance of the Spirit right through the day.

"I thank my God, I speak with tongues more than ye all: yet in the church I had rather speak five words with my understanding, that by my voice I might teach others also, than ten thousand words in an unknown tongue" (1 Corinthians 14:18,19). Many people will come round and say that Paul said he would rather speak five words with the known tongue than ten thousand words without understanding. They will always leave out that part of the sentence, "I thank my God, I speak with tongues more than ye all." Paul was here correcting the excessive speaking in tongues without interpretation, which was not for the edification of the assembly. If there was no interpreter present, they were simply to speak to themselves and to God. Suppose we had someone preaching and we had twenty or thirty people throughout the congregation speaking in tongues. There would be confusion. The people who attend the meeting would rather have five words of edification, consolation and comfort than ten thousand words without understanding.

Because you feel a touch of the Spirit does not mean you are obliged to speak in tongues. The Lord will give you a sound mind so that you will hold your body in perfect order for the edification of the church. But Paul here says that he spake in tongues more than they all; and, as it is evident that the Corinthian church was given to this thing very considerably, he certainly must have been speaking in tongues both day and night. He was so edified by this wonderful, supernatural means of being built up, that he could go to the church, and preaching in a manner so that they could all understand him, he would marvelously edify the saints.

"In the law it is written, With men of other tongues and other lips will I speak unto this people; and yet for all that will they not hear me, saith the Lord. Wherefore tongues are for a sign, not to them that believe, but to them that believe not" (1 Corinthians 14:21,22). There are many who call themselves believers who are extremely unbelieving. One of the unbelieving "believers" was a minister who lived in Sheffield, England. A man gave him a check and told him to go and take a vacation. This man also gave him my name and address; so, when he got to Bradford, he began to inquire about me. He was warned against me as one of the "tongues people" and was told to be very careful and not to be taken in, for the whole thing was of the devil. He said, "They will not take me in; I know too much for them to take me in."

He was quite run down and needed rest; and when he came he said, "A friend of yours sent me; is it all right?" I replied, "Yes, you are welcome." But we could do nothing with that man. It was impossible. Talk? You never heard anyone talk like him. It was talk, talk, talk, talk. I said, "Let him alone, he will surely finish some day." We had dinner, and he talked through dinner time; we had the next meal, and he talked through that.

It was our Friday night meeting for those seeking the Baptism, and the room began to fill with people; and still he talked. No one could get an edge in. He lodged himself in a place where he could not be disturbed by those coming in. I said, "Brother, you will have to stop now, we are going to pray." As a general thing we had some singing before going to prayer; but this time it was different. It was God's order. We immediately went to prayer and as soon as we began to pray, two young women began speaking in tongues. And this minister—it was all so strange to him—moved from one to the other to hear what they were saying. In a little while he said, "May I go to my room?" I said, "Yes, brother, if you wish." So he went to his room and we had a wonderful time.

We went to bed about eleven o'clock or so and at half-past three in the morning this man came to the bedroom door. Knock, knock, "May I come in?" "Yes, come in." He opened the door and said, "He is come, He is come"—holding his mouth, for he could hardly speak in English. I said, "Go back to bed, tell us to-morrow." Tongues are for the unbeliever, and this man was an unbeliever, an unbelieving "believer."

Again and again I have seen conviction come upon people through the speaking in tongues.

The next morning he came down to breakfast and said, "Oh, was not that a wonderful night?" He said, "I know Greek and Hebrew, and those two young women were speaking these languages, one was saying in Greek, 'Get right with God,' and the other was saying the same thing in Hebrew. I knew it was God speaking, and I knew it was not they. I first had to repent. I came in an unbeliever, but I found that God is here. In the night God laid me on the floor for about two hours. I was helpless. Then God broke through." Then he began again to speak in tongues, right over the breakfast table.

God will have witnesses of His mighty power that no man can gainsay. You will have to see that the Holy Spirit will speak through you in tongues and interpretation which will bring conviction to the unbeliever in the open air; and you will find that God will convict by this means.

I will explain to you the most perfect way to receive the gift. Come with me to the second chapter of 2 Kings and I will show you a man receiving a gift. Elijah had been mightily used of God in calling down fire and in other miracles; and Elisha is moved with a great spirit of covetousness to have this man's gifts. You can be very covetous for the gifts of the Spirit and God will allow it. When Elijah said to him, "I want you to stop at Gilgal," Elisha said, "As the Lord liveth and as thy soul liveth, I will not leave thee." There was no stopping him. When Elijah wanted Elisha to stop at Jericho he said in substance, "I am not stopping." The man that stops gets nothing. Oh, don't stop at Jericho; don't stop at Jordan; don't stop anywhere when God would have you move on into all of His fullness that He has for you.

They came to Jordan and Elijah took his mantle and smote the waters. They divided; and Elijah and Elisha went over on dry ground. Elijah turned to Elisha and said in substance, "Look here, what do you want?" Elisha was wanting what he was going to have, and you may covet all that God says that you shall have. Elisha said, "I pray thee, let a double portion of thy spirit be upon me." This was the plowboy, who had washed the hands of his master; but his spirit got so big that he purposed in his heart that, when Elijah stepped off the scene, he would be put into his place.

Elijah said, "Thou hast asked a hard thing: nevertheless, if thou see me when I am taken from thee, it shall be so unto thee." May God help you never to stop persevering till you get what you want. Let your aspiration be large and your faith rise until you are wholly on fire for God's best.

Onward they go, and as one steps, the other steps with him. He purposed to keep his eye on his master until the last. It took a chariot of fire and horses of fire to part them asunder, and Elijah went up by a whirlwind into heaven. I can fancy I hear Elisha crying out, "Father Elijah, drop that mantle!" And it came down. Oh, I can see it lowering, lowering and lowering. Elisha took all of his own clothes and rent them in two pieces, and then he took up the mantle of Elijah. I do not believe that, when he put on that other mantle, he felt any difference in himself; but when he came to Jordan, he took the mantle of Elijah and smote the waters and said, "Where is the Lord God of Elijah?" And the waters parted and he went on dry ground. And the sons of the prophets said, "The spirit of Elijah doth rest upon Elisha."

It is like receiving a gift; you don't know that you have it till you act in faith. As you ask, BELIEVE.